MAKING IT...
OR NOT

The *real* journey told by professional players

MAKING IT...
OR NOT

The real journey told by professional players

AMY SCHEMBRI

First published in 2024 by Fair Play Publishing
PO Box 4101, Balgowlah Heights, NSW 2093, Australia

www.fairplaypublishing.com.au

ISBN: 978-1-923236-17-2
ISBN: 978-1-923236-18-9

© Amy Schembri 2024
The moral rights of the author have been asserted.

All rights reserved. Except as permitted under the
Australian Copyright Act 1968 (for example, a fair dealing for the
purposes of study, research, criticism or review),
no part of this book may be reproduced, stored in a retrieval system,
communicated or transmitted in any form or by any means without
prior written permission from the Publisher.

Design and typesetting by Leslie Priestley
Photographs supplied by the featured players or Amy Schembri

All inquiries should be made to the Publisher via hello@fairplaypublishing.com.au

A catalogue record of this book is available from the National Library of Australia.

Contents

Preface	vii
Introduction: Lace Up Your Boots Here	1
Meet the Players	3
Part 1: Junior Days	10
Fun! Joy! Excitement! Maybe a few nerves…	11
Part 2: Youth Days	31
Part 3: Going Pro	64
Part 4: Life After Football	115
The Parents Role	123
Let's Talk Football	137
Acknowledgements	138
About the Author	141

*To my sons, Jai, Levi and Dion,
who I love unconditionally and who
I will always be there
for during life's highs and lows.*

Preface

When I was born, my dad still played football and not long afterwards my brother put on a pair of boots for the first time. My family was, and still is, obsessed with the game, and as a result, much of my childhood was spent travelling from one pitch to another. Everyone played, including my dad, brother, uncles, cousins and even my grandfather, and when they couldn't anymore, many of them coached.

Growing up, our Saturday nights were spent preparing for game day. We still had an enjoyable social life, but watching football on television, analysing games, and listening to the passion in my dad's voice as he prepared my brother for his upcoming match was a weekly ritual. The car ride home was no different as further analysis took place.

There were ongoing conversations around positioning and tactics, and often a lively debate about what worked well and what didn't. Consequently, I took in more than I ever set out to, absorbing the technical details as well as my family's love for the game. I knew the 'off-side' rule by the time I reached five years old. This placed me in good stead when I decided to take to the pitch as a teenager. Fast-forward a few decades, and now my nephews and three sons play, and they love it just as much as the generations preceding them.

Here I am again, driving from one pitch to another, watching them play, analysing their performances, and cheering them on. I'm anxiously observing their football journey play out before me, much like my mother did when my brother was on the pitch. While it is my family's sport of choice, admittedly, it isn't an easy sport to navigate or succeed in. I have witnessed and shared the many ups and downs associated with it from different perspectives—first as a daughter, then as a little sister, and now as a mum.

As someone sitting on the sidelines, I have witnessed families distraught due to non-selection or being dropped, including (but not limited to) a teenager hitting himself, kids crying uncontrollably and experiencing panic attacks. Anxiety and depression sometimes follow. I have also witnessed kids develop a level of resilience I thought impossible for their age, putting more fire in their belly to prove selectors wrong, and seen these setbacks lead to soaring confidence. Players are likely to experience an array of feelings during their football careers, ranging from suffering and devastation to elation and unimaginable success.

There is no telling what the next season will hold, but I can guarantee you that every player experiences some level of success and some level of disappointment. I know this because it's happened to *every single member* of my family. Whether you're a talented athlete playing in one of the world's biggest leagues or a kid who's in it for fun like I was, there are no exceptions. That is sport. That is football.

Despite my family's commitment to the game and my years of experience, I'm still baffled by how many of our kids (some as young as eight) who are forced to deal with extreme levels of emotion without any knowledge of what to expect or any understanding of situations like trials and penalty shoot-outs. As a parent of three football players, I have experienced dramatic and ongoing highs and lows with my kids. Navigating through the tough times is hard for any player and their parents. All children in sport need coping skills. They need to know the lows are inevitable, normal even, and that they can and will feel successful again. Lows are part of the game, and they don't mean you give up or take them personally. It's important to know young players develop at different paces too.

Despite the high level of success all the players interviewed in this book have achieved, kids in football need to know that none of them experienced a smooth and stress-free road to the top. That road doesn't exist. *Making It . . . or Not* normalises the rejections and setbacks for players of all ages and abilities. They will learn patience, persistence and resilience directly from their idols—coping skills I wish many of my family members had when they went through their journeys.

This book also allows you to identify and determine your definition of 'making it'. Success may mean having fun and making lifelong friends, or it may be playing in one of the highest leagues in the world. The players interviewed here paint a realistic picture of what it's truly like at different levels so that you are equipped with the knowledge to make your own decisions.

In reading this book, you'll learn things you never knew about each of the players: their sacrifices, hardships, injuries and unique trajectories. From the conversations that started in my family's living room as a child to the ones I'm having with my own kids, this book is meant to help parents and kids to navigate a football journey and help each player identify what they truly want for themselves.

Amy Schembri

Introduction:
Lace Up Your Boots Here

"I don't understand, Mum. I worked so hard, gave every game my all, practised at home, never missed a training session. My coach told me I was playing well. How did Joe and Ben make it, and I didn't? It doesn't make sense. I'm not good enough."

Tears rolled down his face as Jase let his disappointment show for not being selected, with each sentence broken by heartfelt gasps of breath. His dreams of playing at an elite level appeared to be slipping farther and farther away—forever, it must have seemed to him. He was only eight years old.

Has this happened to you or a friend of yours? How did it make you feel? What did you say to your friend?

Over the course of the next two weeks, there were moments of silence where Jase appeared to drown in his own thoughts — internalising and processing. I wondered what he was thinking. Would he overcome this obstacle without lasting damage? Would he ever step onto the pitch again? He asked me, his mum, several questions, seeking understanding, comfort and anything to help him sleep better.

Many children fight each year during the trial period to keep their spot in their team for the following season. The season just gone has been long enough for players to have formed strong friendships, and many have begun to feel like they have taken their first step to living their dream. The thought of being dropped can feel scary and devastating.

Did you know tryouts are tough on your parents too?

The truth is, sometimes we just don't know what to do or say, but that's why I've written this book—for every player to get a clear idea of what it really takes to 'make it'. By reading the stories of your heroes, you will come to understand that it's normal to have ups and downs in football. Also, it can help you decide what is most important to you.

This book is divided into four parts. Each part represents a particular time in a football career to ensure you gain detailed insight into each period. Throughout the book, I interview players who are currently playing at a professional level, retired from playing, or close to playing at a professional level but didn't quite get there for reasons you will discover. Best of all, you will find out about their journeys, from junior days up until the day they hung up their boots, including their feelings and the strategies they used to navigate them.

At the end of the book, you are provided with a series of questions to consider. They are all designed to encourage you to have a discussion with your parents, coaches and teammates. There is also a chapter dedicated to your parents. Your parents will benefit from this book too because the interviewed players explain how they can best support you in your ambitions. An A-League coach and a psychologist also have some ideas to share.

Challenging times in sport can be difficult, but they happen to everyone. Reading this book will prepare you for those times so that you can go on to live your best sporting life, whatever it looks like for you.

So, let's get you ready, shall we? It's time to lace up your boots!

Statistic

A staggering less than 1 per cent will 'make it' as a professional footballer.

Definition of 'Making it'

To accomplish something or to become successful. It means you've achieved success or reached a goal you've been working towards. It could be in sport, school, music or anything else you're passionate about. It's all about doing well and feeling proud of what you've accomplished.

Meet the Players

The players who share their story in this book are not featured in any particular order, and while they recount all the highs and lows making their journeys explicitly theirs, the period in which they experienced them may differ. This means that both their interviews and the amount of content within each part of the book vary.

Each player provides you with a strong message or theme:

- Melissa and Adriana Taranto remind you to continually find the joy in playing and remember to have fun.
- Joshua Risdon teaches you the importance of having an identity outside of football.
- Chloe Logarzo shows you that sometimes it's important to step away for a while to rekindle your love of the game.
- Emily Gielnik is proof that resilience and hard work is key to success, no matter what career you're pursuing.
- Callum Nicholas helps you to realise you are bigger than the game and that there is more to life than football. Recovering and then resetting is sometimes necessary.
- Diogo Ferreira is an example of how the definition of 'making it' can look different for everyone.

While they all teach you separate valuable lessons, in the end, one common message they all share is that no road to success is ever a straight line.

MEET CALLUM NICHOLAS

"By the time I was eight years old, I could have signed for Manchester United, Manchester City, Bolton or Everton.

I got my love back for playing football and I wasn't playing in the highest league."

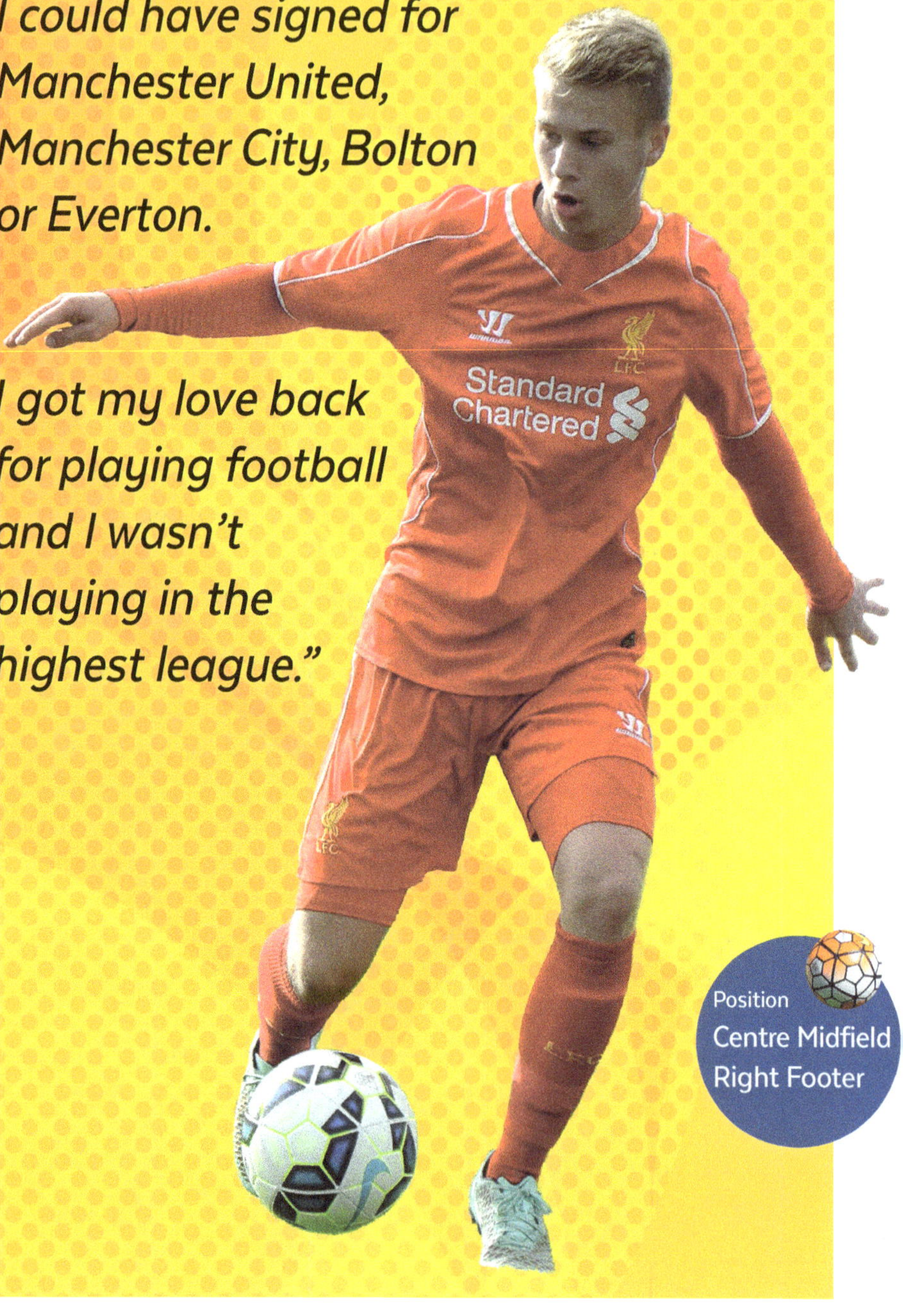

Position
Centre Midfield
Right Footer

MEET CHLOE LOGARZO

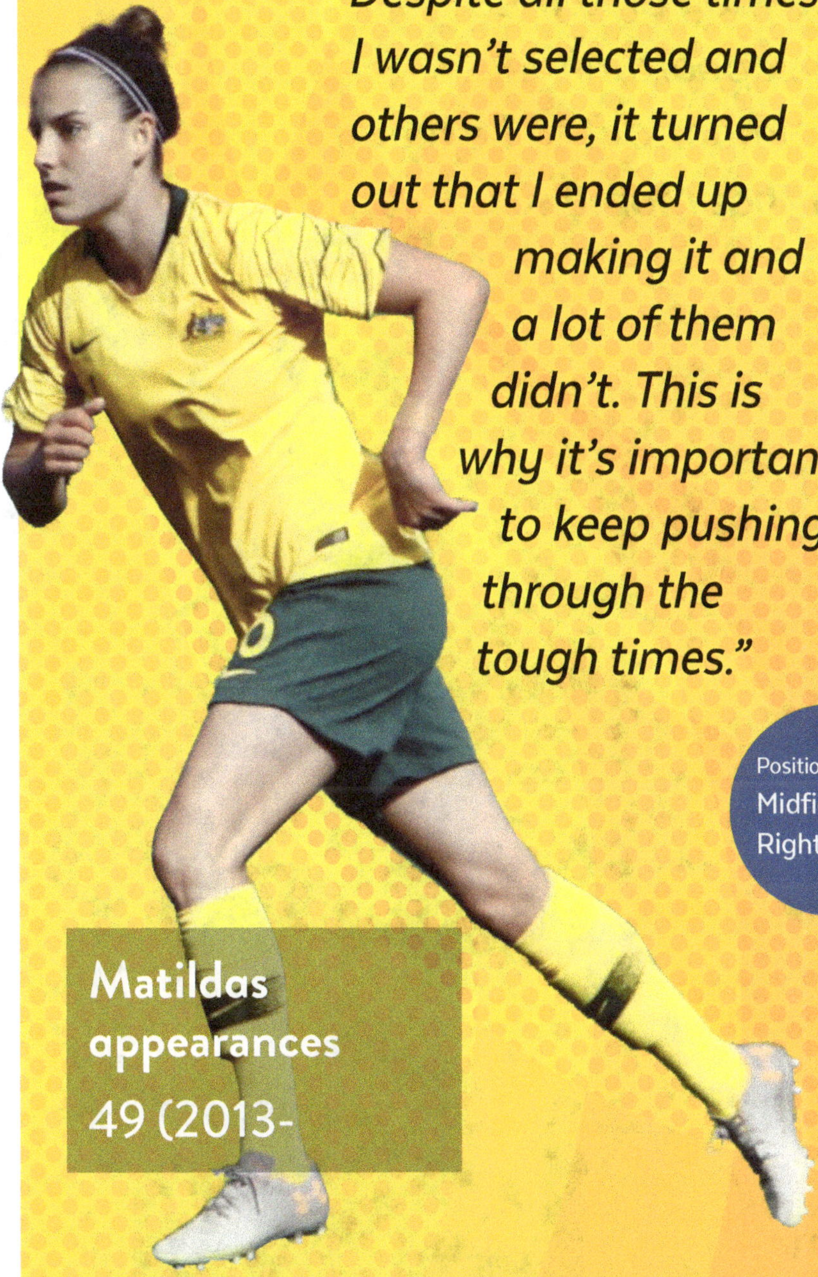

"Despite all those times I wasn't selected and others were, it turned out that I ended up making it and a lot of them didn't. This is why it's important to keep pushing through the tough times."

Position
Midfielder
Right Footer

Matildas appearances
49 (2013-

MEET
DIOGO FERREIRA

"You may only get one opportunity. It's important to be ready for that moment."

Position
Defensive Midfielder
Right Footer

Australia U-23 appearances
7 (2010-2013)

A·LEAGUE PREMIERS 2014

Coach

MEET
EMILY GIELNIK

Position
Striker
Right Footer

"I believe there are two types of people, those who are told 'no' and accept it and those who are told 'no' and do something about it."

Matildas appearances
54 (2012-

MEET
JOSH RISDON

Position
Right Back
Right Footer

"I walked into the change rooms, saw my yellow jersey hanging with my name on the back and thought 'Wow'. There are no words to describe that feeling."

Socceroo appearances
15 (2015-2019)

A·LEAGUE
CHAMPIONS
2022

MEET
MELISSA & ADRIANA TARANTO

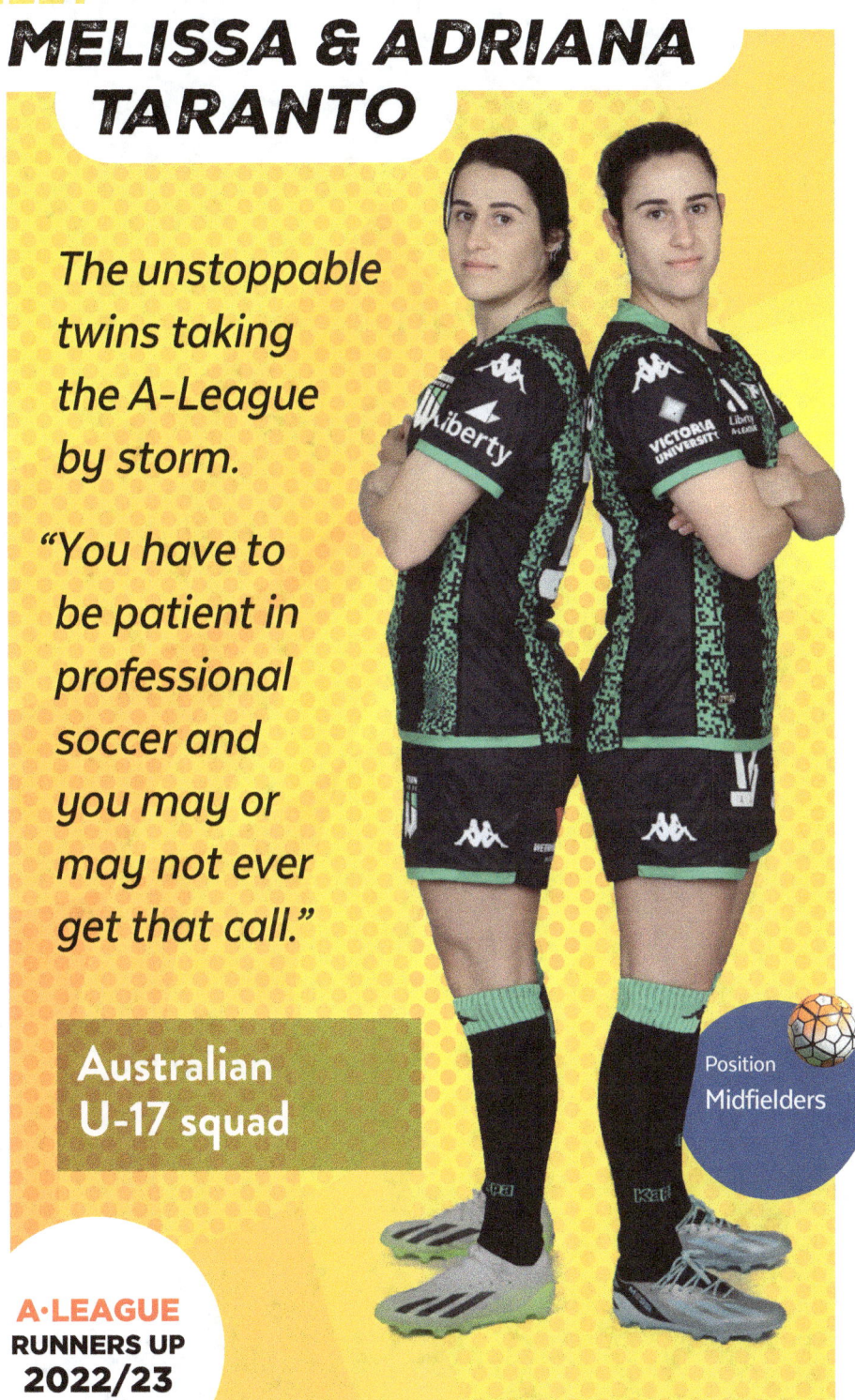

The unstoppable twins taking the A-League by storm.

"You have to be patient in professional soccer and you may or may not ever get that call."

Australian U-17 squad

Position: **Midfielders**

A·LEAGUE RUNNERS UP 2022/23

Part 1:
Junior Days

Fun! Joy! Excitement! Maybe a few nerves . . .

These are the words describing the moment you step out onto a pitch for the first time. Players slip on their brand-new boots, all shiny and bright, smelling of unworn leather, and the feeling is nothing short of sensational. Friendships begin to form with teammates, and you soon know how good it feels to be part of a community. Passion and love for the game ignites and begins to grow, rapidly.

Years later, professional players still talk about how they felt and what attracted them to football in the first place. They remember what they did when faced with challenges early on. For these athletes, quitting was never an option, because their love and passion for the game outweighed any setback.

MAKING IT...OR NOT

Melissa and Adriana Taranto

*"Pure fun. We loved being part of a team...
not just for the physical aspect,
but for the self-esteem and life lessons."*

Why football?
Both: We found it fun! We had an older brother who played, and we would often attend his training sessions and games. While there, we kicked a ball on the sidelines and other parents would say to ours, "Your daughters are pretty good. You should get them into football too."

    Adriana: I clearly remember the day I turned to Mel and said, *"Why don't we start playing? We should!"* We were eight years old.

    When we asked our dad if we could play, he said, *"Yes. We'll put you in with the boys."* Back then it wasn't popular for a girl to play football. There were no girls' teams, so we had to play with the boys.

What was it like for you both when you started?
Melissa: We started at Moreland Wolves. We had a great coach and really loved playing and getting rough. We weren't scared. Every weekend, we would go out and play well. Sometimes we got knocked down, but we would get straight back up and keep pushing.

Were the boys reluctant to tackle you or get rough because you were girls?
Adriana: At first, the boys held off a bit, but when they realised we could hold our own, they started playing their normal game. We had such a great team, and being a family club, we made a lot of friends there.

Do either of you remember your first game?
Both: No, we don't.

    Adriana: We remember our first uniform and training sessions though. Our uniforms were blue with yellow, and we would train on the side of the pitch.

How would you describe your junior days?
Melissa: Pure fun! We loved being part of a team.

    Adriana: I don't think either of us could play an individual sport. Whenever young kids tell me that they aren't feeling great, I recommend they get themselves into a team sport, not just for the physical aspect but for the self-esteem and life lessons.

PART 1: JUNIOR DAYS

Did either of you experience any 'ups and downs' during your time as junior players?
Adriana: Honestly, through our junior years, we were lucky in that everything went well for us. Eventually, we moved into an all-girls team, first at Essendon Royals and then at Pascoe Vale FC. With both clubs, we played every game and won most of our games and tournaments. It was a positive start to our career.

Melissa: One thing we did encounter though was constant comparisons between the two of us because we are twins. We would hear people say, "Adriana is stronger, but Mel is faster." This would sometimes trigger me to compare myself to my sister, which caused me to feel some self-doubt. I would often wonder *Who's better?* and think *She's stronger than me. She's better than me.*

Adriana: Looking back on our junior years and considering which one of us the coaches could've or should've played, we were lucky in that we were both in the starting lineup. We didn't suffer any injuries, and we won most games and, consequently, the title.

Our junior years were very enjoyable, and our journeys continued to be that way until we reached the professional stage.

MAKING IT...OR NOT

Joshua Risdon

*"I had to give up playing with my friends
so that I could play at a higher level to better myself,
and as hard as it was, that's what I did."*

Why football?
Josh: It's quite funny. My dad played Aussie Rules Football (AFL) his whole life, so my parents had no knowledge of football. One day, my dad was told that if you want to start your kids in sport, start with football because it's more skills-based, which makes it easier for them to switch to Aussie Rules down the track. My dad did that with my brother and me. I was about six years old at the time. We started to love playing football, and our school friends were on the same team.

I was obsessed. I used to train every morning before school and, when I got home from school, in the backyard. I played football all the time.

For the first few years, I played in my own age group, but by the time I reached the age of nine or ten, I started playing in my older brother's team with his mates.

How did it feel to be told you could play up an age group?
Josh: Yeah, it felt good. I was pretty good for my age. In fact, I would often go and play with my brother's year level at school, so I wanted to step up and play with them on the weekends. They were a talented team. It was a good feeling knowing I could do it. It was a lot tougher, of course, but I believe I needed that.

Did you experience any jealousy from others because you were chosen to play up?
Josh: My brother's team took the game more seriously than my age group did at the time, so I don't think so.

There was one time when I felt bad though. It was the school sports carnival, and I was on the football team. I was in grade six and the PE (physical education) teacher, who coached us, asked me to play in the year seven team because he wanted to win. The year level above me was more serious about sport. I felt bad because I wanted to play with my friends and help them do well too, so I didn't end up doing it.

What was your first club like?
Josh: It was a great club, very family oriented. We would have family nights and be ball boys for the first team on the weekends. It had a great community feel, and that's another reason we loved it.

PART 1: JUNIOR DAYS

How long were you at your first club for?
Josh: I was at the same club from the age of six until twelve years old.

How would you describe your junior days?
Josh: When young, it was all about pure enjoyment. That's what football was for me. I loved sports and playing football. It was all about having fun.

What happened after the age of twelve?
Josh: My brother, who was a very talented player, and I played in our local league in Bunbury, while our friends travelled three hours to Perth and played at a higher level. My brother, who was in year seven, started doing the same thing. Halfway through his first season, I began travelling and training with his team in the hope I would be offered a spot in their league the following season.

By the time I was in year seven, I was playing in Perth too. I would travel there every Thursday night, then play for the team on Sunday. I could still play with my team in Bunbury in between, on Saturday; however, a new rule was introduced that meant we no longer could play for both teams.

What did you decide to do?
Josh: It was the first sacrifice I made. Unbeknownst to me at the time, it was one of many yet to come. I had to give up playing with my friends so that I could play at a higher level to better myself, and as hard as it was, that's what I did. I chose to play with ECU Joondalup and started travelling twice per week to Perth and to games on weekends.

How did your parents accommodate this?
Josh: Mum or Dad would drive my brother and me to Perth on a Thursday, then again on the weekend for our games. My mum was a schoolteacher. She would finish work, pick us up after lunchtime and drive us up.

How did you cope with missing school?
Josh: At first, it wasn't too bad because it was only once per week; however, it got harder when I was in years eight and nine.

At the end of year seven, my brother stopped going. He decided he didn't want to travel anymore. He wanted to come back home and play the game with his mates. He had a group of close-knit friends, who were all very talented players as well, and he missed playing with them. My brother also loved cricket and other sports too.

I, on the other hand, ended up making the State team, so I started training twice a week for that as well. By that time, I trained four to five times per week plus playing on game day. That is why years eight and nine were very tough, and it became taxing on my parents too. My parents spent time away from my siblings as well, and I felt guilty about that.

I travelled to Perth on Mondays and Wednesdays for State training, Thursdays for the club

I played with, then stayed in Perth on the weekend because I attended another development squad session on Saturday and played games on Sunday. We stayed at my grandmother's house, and my parents took turns driving me each weekend. Despite all this, it was during this time I realised I wanted to become a professional football player.

I wasn't the brightest student, and leaving school at lunch on Mondays, Wednesdays and Thursdays probably didn't help. Back then, I didn't care too much about school, but I have since learned how important it is, and I'm studying for a university degree now.

What other sacrifices were you starting to make to pursue football?
Josh: Travelling a lot, and being at football all the time, meant I missed out on a lot regarding school life. I had a couple of friends in high school, but I was never able to make good connections with a large group of friends because I was always at football. At school, I was just known as the kid who played football.

How did you personally cope with the sacrifices and the amount of travel required?
Josh: There were times when I used to say to my mum and dad I didn't want to go to Perth because it got really tiring. My mum and dad never pushed me, but my dad gave me a valuable lesson, one that I will never forget:

One day he came up to me because he noticed I hadn't trained at home in a while, and he said, *"Oh, why don't you go kick the ball and do some juggling?"* I responded with, *"I can't be bothered."* He then pointed out to me I hadn't practised much of late and proceeded to demand I help him dig a hole for some new plumbing he was putting in. He gave me a shovel and explained to me that if I wasn't going to kick a ball, then I needed to learn how to do something else. I started digging a big trench for him so he could do the plumbing. I think I lasted ten minutes before I grabbed a ball and started juggling.

By the end of year nine, after much discussion with my parents, I decided to move to Joondalup in Perth by myself. I was fourteen years old.

How did it feel moving away from your mum, dad and siblings at fourteen?
Josh: When my parents and I made a collective decision, we spoke about how that was going to look. A friend of my dad's was a bachelor. They studied together when they were younger and had remained friends. He was a big football fan too. We arranged to

PART 1: JUNIOR DAYS

get an apartment I shared with him.

It was near the new school I attended. I remember feeling doubtful, and I knew I was going to miss my family a lot, but I was so focused on becoming a professional player that I didn't let that stop me. At the time, I didn't realise how big of a move it was.

Once my mum and dad finished helping me settle in at Perth, they left. I struggled for the first two weeks they were gone. It was tough. I cried myself to sleep every night during the first week. I felt so lonely. Going to a new school was daunting too.

Fortunately, my parents would alternate coming up every weekend so I would get to see one of them. That was great, but it was hard saying goodbye over and over again.

Being away from my brothers, who I'm very close to, was hard as well. We did everything together growing up, and I missed them very much. Being away from my family was tough.

How did you look after yourself?
Josh: I'm grateful for the family friend I lived with. He became my guardian for three years, and without him, I don't think my parents would have allowed me to leave.

Moving away from home forced me to learn how to look after myself. I had to grow up. I did my own cooking, cleaning, washing, grocery shopping, and getting myself ready and off to school. I had no choice but to become independent very quickly.

Did you make some new friends through school?
Josh: I had a couple of friends who I already knew going to the school I chose to go to. They were teammates. Once I got to school, it was great. I made a lot of friends quickly, which helped.

While playing for ECU Joondalup, or the State team, did you struggle to get game time?
Josh: No, but my preferred position at the time was a struggle to break into. I played in the midfield for my club, but when I went to trial for the State team, I soon realised there was no chance I was going to be picked to play in that position. I was placed in the right back position, which I went along with at the time. Funnily enough, when I eventually 'made it', it was as a right back. Had I been adamant about playing in the midfield, and not been open to playing wherever the coach wanted to put me, I probably wouldn't have made the team.

Do you love the right back position now?
Josh: Yeah, I do. It's just very comfortable for me because I've been playing that position for so long. It's good because, these days, you're not always restricted to staying back. You can move up the pitch a lot more, so it's a diverse role. I really enjoy it.

At some point, did you find it difficult to keep up with all your football commitments?
Josh: At the end of year nine, I tried out and got into NTC (National Training Centre), which is an elite development squad for my age group. That was on top of being in the State team. I was required to train almost every night, then we would play in a league on the weekend. I became very committed to NTC. As a result, I had to leave my ECU Joondalup club.

Do you recommend training that much?
Josh: Yes. It prepares you to become a professional. I sometimes see National Premier League (NPL) teams training twice per week, which is fine, but when some of those players break into the professional league and switch to training five days per week, they struggle a bit.

In the State squad, did you witness teammates getting dropped or deselected in a cutthroat environment?
Josh: Due to the level of competitiveness, it was tough. Our squad consisted of players from three different age groups selected from different clubs. Consequently, we witnessed some of our teammates get cut from the NTC squad. They would be shattered.

When the State season restarted, we went back to our State teams and saw those players again. They would try so hard, and you could see the desperation they had to get back into the NTC squad. Some would and others wouldn't. There were boys who fell away as a result, and some stuck around and continued to push. Many of them ended up playing in the A-League and having successful careers.

PART 1: JUNIOR DAYS

Chloe Logarzo

*"I lost all feeling from my neck down and thought
I was never going to play football again."*

How old were you when you started playing football, and what was your first club?
Chloe: I started when I was five years old. I played for Carlingford Redbacks, which was down the road from where I lived. My parents probably started me in this club because it was very convenient. There's no other sport I have ever played.

What drew you to the sport in the first place?
Chloe: I have one parent who is Italian and one who is Scottish, so both my parents are lovers of football. My dad played and my grandfather loved it. Because of my family history, I always felt it was the natural choice. Typically, growing up, Dad was my coach and Mum my team manager. I really loved playing.

How would you describe your junior days, and did you experience any setbacks?
Chloe: At eleven years old, I was involved in an accident on the field. I got pushed in the back, and the ball hit me on the top of my head. I was paralysed for eight hours. I lost all feeling from my neck down and thought I was never going to play football again. That was a very scary moment, but it didn't deter me. The following week, a representative scout came out and watched one of our games. At that time, I played in the boys/mixed league, but because of that game, I was selected to play representative football in an all-girls' team.

What was it like making the transition to a new club?
Chloe: That was the first time I played in an U12 all-girls' team, and it was with North West Sydney Koalas. I stayed with this club from U12 to U15. I truly enjoyed my time.

While there, I also attended a private school. One of the girls I met playing indoor football told me she attended Hill Sports High School, a sports academy. I really wanted to go, so I applied. My mum hid the acceptance letter from me for approximately four months because she didn't want me to leave the private school I was at; however, from year seven onwards, I started attending that school, which is when I started taking football more seriously.

Do you think you were a good player from a young age?
Chloe: No. I was okay, but I wasn't a standout player. I was tiny. I weighed forty

kilograms. I ran a lot and put a lot of hard work into the game, but I don't believe I was technically good.

What was your training schedule like?
Chloe: When I first started playing, I was training two nights a week, then it increased to three nights. When I changed schools, I started training every day because football was one of my subjects. The football program was intense. My coach went on to become the Sydney FC coach, then the national team coach. This high school developed five Matildas!

What was your school coach like?
Chloe: He taught me a lot about football, and as a result, I started making strides in terms of development.

What strides did you make?
Chloe: There was a program at NSWIS (New South Wales Institute of Sport). This program consisted of a group of girls from New South Wales who were chosen to represent that State in a national tournament. I finally got into this program after being rejected after so many trials previously. When a coach knows you and your game, it can help open doors, but you have to earn your place on every team and take every opportunity.

PART 1: JUNIOR DAYS

Emily Gielnik

"I would run past the other players and clean up the scraps. I had an innate hunger to do everything, but I was never a selfish player. I would often gift goals to others who struggled a bit more."

How old were you when you began playing football?
Emily: I was twelve years old, which is a lot older than many others. Initially, my mum didn't want me to play football because she thought it was too rough, so my first love was basketball. I always played football with the boys at school though and was part of the boys' team.

I didn't have any skill or talent, but I had willingness, effort and energy. I was obsessed with all things sport related. I played anything and everything. After years of begging my mum to allow me to play football, I finally got into an U12 football team in Brisbane at a club called Redlands United.

What was your first season like with that club?
Emily: In my first season, I remember turning up to trials and there were two coaches. One of the coaches said to the other, *"I don't care who you choose for your team, but that girl is in mine."* He was referring to me, and I didn't find out about this until a year after it happened.

In terms of performance, I scored approximately sixty goals that year, and all of them were with my toes [*Emily laughs*].

I had no skills, no idea how to do 'step-overs', nothing. I was just fast, had goal-scoring instincts and was super competitive.

Would you say you could read the game from a young age?
Emily: A little bit, but the thing I had most was athleticism. I would run past the other players and clean up the scraps. I had an innate hunger to do everything, but I was never a selfish player. I would often gift goals to others who struggled a bit more.

How long did you play with this club for?
Emily: I played with this club and this team for a few years, then I began to get chosen to play in 'Rep' sides. While all of this sounds positive, one thing I did struggle with during my junior years was getting selected for the State team. I was never picked.

Was that tough for you?
Emily: I don't know if it was a coincidence, but every time I went to trial for the State team, I would roll my ankle. I always played well though, but for some reason, I would watch all my friends get selected, and I was not. It was humiliating for me because we would all sit in a circle while the selectors would call out the names of those who were chosen. My name would never get called.

How did you cope with that given you were so young?
Emily: I was fine, but I do remember one time when I quit for a year because of not being picked. I was fourteen years old and players from my regional team received letters offering them a spot at the Queensland Academy of Sport (QAS). All my friends got an offer, and I didn't. I didn't know anything about it until one of my friends asked if I got 'the letter'. I responded with *"What letter?*

What was this QAS program you wanted to get into like?
Emily: It offered players a full-time program where they were required to train five days a week, plus two early morning gym sessions, and a game against boys every Wednesday. I felt devastated when I didn't get an offer, so much so I decided not to play for a year. I was so angry. I was young and felt I deserved it.

Did you do anything else instead?
Emily: I played every other sport you can think of at school, including football. I just didn't play football outside of school. At school, I was one of the best players, and I remember my sports teachers having so much faith in me. They were the ones who said to me, *"You will play with the Matildas one day."* I didn't believe them back then, particularly after having experienced so many setbacks.

How important is it to have at least one person believe in you?
Emily: Very important. Funny thing is, I found out recently my dad used to drive to the QAS and watch the girls train. When I asked him why he did that, he told me it was because he felt I deserved to be there, that he knew I was at that level. I was a bit embarrassed, and I don't know how long he did that for, but it shows me how much he believed in me as well.

PART 1: JUNIOR DAYS

Callum Nicholas

"Do you know who United have signed?"
I responded with, "I don't know. Ronaldo?" He then replied,
"No. They want to sign you!"

How old were you when you started playing?
Callum: I remember watching home videos from when my sisters and I were kids, and there's footage of me in a pram, always holding a football. I kicked a ball from the moment I could walk, but I started playing in an U8 team at five years old. My first club was Urmston Town FC.

Do you remember your first game, and what was that like?
Callum: My first game was when I went to watch some of my friends play in a tournament, and they were short of players, so they invited me to join in. All the players were two or three years older than me. I remember going onto the pitch, and everyone was just running after the ball. The game went to penalties. I refused to take one because I thought, if I miss it, my teammates, who were all older than me, would get mad at me at school the next day. The next season, I signed for the team and played with them until I was nine years old.

How do you feel you performed in those early days?
Callum: I felt like I did well. I could tell from a young age I was a decent player. In fact, I was scouted for Manchester City at five years old, then Manchester United at six years old.

You were scouted at a very young age. What did that look like for you?
Callum: The big clubs have centres all over the UK. You could have thirty to forty players in the northwest region and thirty to forty players in the southern region attending what they call the 'Satellite Program'. I would train with Manchester City and Manchester United every week, then play for my local team on the weekend.

What was training like?
Callum: You turn up to training each week, and if you're good, you get invited back the following week. You had to perform consistently. I saw some kids come once or twice, then I never saw them again. This continued until such time as they felt you were ready to attend the real academy.

I was travelling between Manchester City and Manchester United weekly, but I hated going to Manchester City because I'm a United fan [*Callum laughs*].

Was it a program to help them identify talent from a young age?
Callum: Yes, then when you reach eight years old, these big clubs decide who they want to sign for the actual football club. Legally, players can't sign until they're nine years old.

Who did you sign with first?
Callum: I trained most nights, juggling between Manchester United, Manchester City and eventually Bolton too, and I still played with my local team on the weekend. I was transparent with all the clubs and told them what I was doing. Until you're signed, the clubs don't have control over who you're allowed to train and play with, and they were fine with it. I think the fact I was honest with them helped.

By the time I was eight years old, I could have signed with Manchester United, Manchester City, Bolton or Everton. My dad decided on Manchester United because I was always good at passing, and I could read the game well, which is what Manchester City focused on, whereas Manchester United focused more on footwork and dribbling.

How did it feel to sign with Manchester United?
Callum: I remember my dad took me to the United ground, and he asked me, *"Do you know who United have signed?"* I responded with, *"I don't know. Ronaldo?"* He then replied, *"No. They want to sign you!"* One of my best friends from football at the time met us there with his family as he was offered a spot at United too. We were told together. It was a moment I'll never forget.

After you signed at the age of nine, how did that change your life and circumstances?
Callum: Once I signed for Manchester United, I wasn't allowed to play in tournaments with my local team anymore. I still went and played in a few though, hoping no one would find out, which I don't think they ever did. On one occasion, Marcus Rashford, who was on my team and signed with United at the same time as me, played in a tournament with his local team against me and my team. Thankfully, neither of us ever said anything.

What was that game like against Marcus and his team?
Callum: We played against each other in the semi-final. We kicked off, and he just ran through our entire team and scored. Then we kicked off, and I did the same to his team. We ended up winning that game. After the game, an Everton scout, who also scouted

PART 1: JUNIOR DAYS

Wayne Rooney, went up to my dad at the end of the game and told him I was ten times better than Rooney was at nine.

To be honest, I think Marcus and I were the two best players in that United team at the time. As you get older, though, the competition becomes harder and harder. From the age of nine through thirteen, clubs bring players in from all over, including London. By the time you're fourteen, clubs are allowed to start bringing players in from places like Brazil. You are competing with kids from all over the world, particularly at a big club like United.

What was that sort of pressure like for you?
Callum: I always felt like my position was threatened when new players came through. I had to perform consistently to keep my spot in the team. I learned this from a very young age.

How often was your contract reviewed?
Callum: It was reviewed every two years.

Did you witness any players being told their contract was not going to be renewed?
Callum: Yes, loads of players. To be fair, you can tell which players are struggling though, particularly when you're young. As you get older, it gets harder to identify. Every player from the age of fourteen is a good player, so by then it often comes down to what traits the club is looking for.

Often, you would see a player who you think is very talented not get offered a contract, and you would be shocked by it. It doesn't mean they aren't good enough; it just means they didn't have that one specific thing they were looking for. It could be something as simple as height.

Tell us more about that time at Manchester United as a junior.
Callum: From the age of eight to ten years, one other player and myself were the standouts at the time. We were often asked to play in games in different locations. We trained four times per week; however, when I was nine, my mum was diagnosed with cancer.

I'm so sorry to hear that. How did you cope?
Callum: I knew my mum was ill, but I wasn't told about her actual diagnosis because my parents didn't want to distract me. By the time I was eleven, she passed away. I was playing for United at the time. In fact, the day my mum passed away was the same day Manchester United and Barcelona played in the Champions League final. We were supposed to have a party at our house that night, but when I came home from being out,

my dad told me we had to go to the hospital and that Mum wasn't going to make it.

In the same year, my grandmother had a stroke, my grandfather was diagnosed with cancer, and at the end of that year, my other grandfather suffered from a brain aneurysm and passed away on New Year's Eve. On the day of his funeral, my other grandfather passed away. A few months later, we received a call that another relative died as well.

My grandmother had to move in with us, and my dad slept on the sofa bed. A year after she moved in, she passed away too. Between the ages of ten to thirteen, I lost five close family members. I didn't return to school or football until approximately eight months after my mum passed away. It was a very tough time for my family.

What was it like when you first returned to football after such a difficult time?
Callum: I had just come back after being gone for eight months, dealing with the loss of my mum, and after two weeks, we had our individual performance review meeting. A new coach who had come on board listed all my faults to my dad, including that I couldn't dribble. I knew I was unfit too. I was U12 or U13 by this stage, and I struggled a lot that season. I remember not feeling wanted.

At what point did things start to turn around for you?
Callum: By the time I was fourteen years old, I had new coaches that were able to get the best out of me. They were professional and pushed me during training. They told me they thought I was one of the best midfielders in England. They helped lift my confidence again.

As a result, I began playing consistently well, and I became one of the best players with United.

That's impressive. What happened from there?
Callum: From the age of eleven to fifteen, you can be asked to attend a school affiliated with the football club. This means you are taken out of school during the day to attend training. The players chosen to be part of this trained more than the other players. I wasn't in this at the time as I had just come back after the loss of my mum; however, Marcus Rashford and Axel Tuanzebe were in the program.

The players asked to join the school are the players they want to nurture to take the next step. When I was fifteen and doing well, my coaches must have been telling others I was a good player. I remember famous coach Sir Alex Ferguson came to watch one of my games. We played against West Bromwich Albion, and I scored. Afterwards he asked my coaches why I didn't get taken out of school to attend training during the day.

On the way home, I received a phone call, and from then on, I was taken out of school for training on Mondays and Tuesdays as well.

PART 1: JUNIOR DAYS

Did that make you feel proud?
Callum: Yeah, it did. I must admit the club was good. When my mum and my grandparents passed away, I got letters from Sir Alex Ferguson, and they sent representatives from the club to attend the funeral as well. Brian McClair, who used to play for Manchester United in the first team, attended.

Having to leave school each week, how did you keep up with your studies?
Callum: I left at twelve o' clock on Mondays and Tuesdays. To be fair, I was a good student. At the time, another player named Cameron Borthwick-Jackson, who was a year above me, was doing the same thing as me. He ended up playing many games in the Premier League with Manchester United.

Anyway, it started off being Mondays only, but then I passed my Science GCSE (General Certificate of Secondary Education) a year early, so I was able to leave on Tuesdays to train too. Because I was doing well at school and keeping up with my work, it was fine.

What happened if you didn't keep up with your schoolwork?
Callum: I never got to that point. I didn't want to find out.
The following year is more critical, though, because not only are you doing the rest of your GCSEs, but it's also when clubs start offering scholarships; that's the biggest year when players are trying to 'make it'.
At what age does this happen?

Callum: Scholarships are offered to U16s, and by the age of seventeen or eighteen, school is finished, and football becomes your job.

Diogo Ferreira

"I would kick the ball against the wall, the fence and the window. I had no structure. I had no cones. All I had was a ball and whatever I could find. I would spend hours until my mum would tell me to come inside. To me, you either have the passion or you don't."

How old were you when you first began playing football?
Diogo: I started playing at the age of eight.

Why did you choose football as your sport?
Diogo: Football was in my family, but I also used to do athletics. I was quite good and would win a lot. I would participate in regional events and often come first. After winning, I would be a bit cheeky and throw my medal at my parents. That's when my parents thought it was time to put me into a team sport.

What was it like, the first time you put football boots on?
Diogo: Funnily enough, I was very confident. The first session I had we played 'numbers football'. This is when the coach calls out 'number one' or 'number two', etc., then you go up against each other. I can't believe I still remember this, but I turned to the boy next to me, and I said to him, *"Don't worry. I'm good."* I was always playing football at home, so I knew I was going to be okay.

How much did you enjoy your junior days?
Diogo: I really enjoyed my junior days [*Diogo smiles*].

What was your experience like at your first club?
Diogo: I loved it because I simply enjoyed playing. I also felt I was good at it and made some good friends too. Also, the parents got along well, and they formed friendships too. It was a fun time, every bit of it. I stayed at my first club until twelve years old.

Where did you go after that?
Diogo: When I look back on my entire football career, the year I remember the most was the one when I moved clubs at the age of twelve. I remember starting in the B team (Wallabies in the MiniRoos League). Halfway through the season, the coaches were impressed with my performance, approached my dad, and asked him if

I could move into the A team. My dad's response was *"Absolutely not."* He believed I should finish the season with the team I was in. That shows the kind of background I came from.

I didn't have pushy parents. They taught me early on there are bigger things in life than football and being on the A team. I stayed in the B team for the rest of that season, and my dad only allowed me to play in the A team once the season was over. In my first game with the A team, I scored a hat trick.

Looking back, I can honestly say the year I spent in that B team was the most enjoyable time of my life, and I still speak to some of those teammates today. Realistically, there's more to sport than just being in the A team.

What happened in the following few years?
Diogo: As much as I enjoyed my time at my second junior club, there was one year when I went to a different club. I was in what was probably the best team at that club in my age group at the time. I was very small, and my teammates had already had their growth spurts. Some are still the same size as adults, so I struggled to get any game time, and I remember my teammates being selected for State teams. Even though I would try out for everything, I never got selected.

I kept hearing I was too small. What made it even harder was not having my dad around because he had moved overseas. My mum looked after me and drove me to training and my games, but I still missed not having my dad around. That was a very difficult year for me. I was thirteen years old.

So, what did you do after that?
Diogo: I went back to the previous club and started enjoying my time. I was selected for the A team again because I was a good player, and by this stage, I had finally grown. My dad was back too.

How much did you practise?
Diogo: We trained twice a week, then had one game on the weekend. Aside from that, I was outside every day. I would get home from school and go outside. It didn't feel like homework. For me, it was just me having fun and trying new things. I would kick the ball against the wall, the fence and the window. I had no structure. I had no cones. All I had was a ball and whatever I could find. I would spend hours until my mum would tell me to come inside.

To me, you either have the passion or you don't. I remember back then we used to rent movies from a local store, and I would always get all the football ones like World Cup '98 or whatever. I would go home and watch those games for hours. No one ever asked me or forced me to. It was my passion.

Did you have to give up other things like school sports?
Diogo: This wasn't an issue when I was growing up because we only trained twice per week, so playing football with school was possible. I would train after school for one hour with my mates and have so much fun. Those were really good times. Unbelievable. It was even fun being on the bus with my school team to attend inter-school sports events.

Now, it's harder for young kids because they train three to four days and football is being taken more seriously at school now too. The kids need to be careful of 'overload'.

I did give up athletics, though, because there wasn't enough time anymore.

Did you ever witness teammates being deselected or dropped?
Diogo: Not really. There were trials at the start of the year for new kids, but it wasn't as difficult as it is now. I mean, now you even have to put in 'expressions of interest'. I believe there is a place for every kid, although I support the A and B structure because you want kids to be playing at a level suited to them. You want a structure allowing kids to push themselves, or to have something to aspire to, but if you put a child who doesn't have the ability on an A team, the kid is going to know they are not good enough, feel it and possibly quit. They may even be on the receiving end of negative comments from their teammates.

Parents may sometimes push for their child to be in an A team when they aren't quite ready. They need to think about their child. At the end of the day, even though they may not say it, deep down, the kids know when they are struggling and not ready.

If a kid asked you *"Why should I pick football?",* what would you say?
Diogo: My response to this would be the same regardless of the sport. Whether it's football, basketball or any other sport, if you love it, then play. I think team sports are great because they teach a lot of life lessons, but regardless of which sport you play, you will still get those lessons.

Part 2:
Youth Days

Things start to get a little more serious during the youth stage. This is when you decide what 'making it' means to you. Are you aiming to go pro, or are you in football for the fun and social aspect?

At this time, players begin to ponder their priorities and decide whether they would prefer to play at a community level instead. Either way, it doesn't matter. It's all about determining what makes you the happiest.

The players in this book opted to pursue a football career, so they were faced with a whole new set of challenges. Juggling high school commitments, moving away from family, being passed over or getting selected but feeling nervous are only some of the experiences they talk about. Sometimes, they had to dig deep to find the joy they experienced as a junior player.

Youth Stats

- 169,463 and growing = number of youth players in Australia
  - 73% male
  - 27% female.
- The odds of getting a professional contract are low. We know this. However, studies have shown that if you haven't been recruited into an academy by the age of twelve, it doesn't mean your dream is over.

PART 2: YOUTH DAYS

Melissa and Adriana Taranto

*"It was really difficult going from life as a Young Matilda
to going back to getting up in the morning
and going to English and maths classes. That period of waiting
feels like torture, but that's just how it is."*

How did you both get identified?
Melissa: At the age of fourteen, we were 'identified' by the National Training Centre (NTC). That was the first time we went through a rigorous, trial-based process. At this point, our parents had to sit us down and explain to us we might not both get picked. They wanted us to be prepared for that possibility. That was a very important conversation.

As twin sisters both pursuing a football career, we pushed each other to be the best we could be, but we were also each other's competitor. We both played in the midfield, and at the time of the NTC trials, we were both specifically playing in the number six position, which is defensive midfield.

Adriana: We went to the training sessions, and I didn't worry too much because I'd always felt we made each other better when we were both on the field. We had good chemistry on the pitch, and because of this, we were often chosen together.

Thankfully, we both got picked for NTC. That turned out to be a good program with amazing coaches. We did the Coffs Harbour, Canberra and the Australian Institute of Sport competitions. We won most games, but we always lost to New South Wales. We were asked to play above our age group, and because of this, we got to train and play with the likes of Stephanie Catley (Matilda), Lisa De Vanna (Matilda), and the senior team at the time, even though we were much younger. That was an incredible experience!

Melissa: At the time I remember feeling so scared, to the point I almost didn't want to be there.

People think, *Oh look at that young person who gets to play with the likes of Lisa De Vanna. How lucky is she?* What they don't understand is the pressure and the stress you feel walking into a changeroom with players like them. As fifteen-year-olds, it was immense. At this point, you start to feel like it's not just about having fun in football anymore.

I would sometimes think these elite players must hate me because I've come in as a younger player. I remember wondering what they thought and whether they felt we weren't good enough or that, because of us, their training sessions were going to be boring. I felt so conflicted. On the one hand, I was grateful to be there training with these great players, but the self-doubt kicks in too. All these things ran through my mind.

Luckily, we had each other which made it so much easier. We both went through the motions and feelings together, and we were able to help and encourage each other during the entire process. We acknowledge it's rare to have that.

What happened from there?
Adriana: We were both invited to go to the U17s Young Matildas' camp. Mum and Dad had to sit us down again and have the same conversation with us about this being another big step and the possibility of only one of us getting selected.

Melissa: When we first got to Canberra for the camp, we were split up. I was in a room with someone else that night, and I recall crying myself to sleep. It was the first time we slept away from our parents. On top of that, my usual teammates and sister weren't with me.

It was a very professional camp. We were given a strict schedule to follow. The schedule detailed where we had to be and when for each of the different training sessions. We were only sixteen years old at the time.

Adriana: We had to find our way to the football pitch.

Melissa: The craziest thing—and this is something I love about football—is that I went from feeling like I hated the situation, being by myself and not knowing anyone, to getting on the training pitch the very next day with a bunch of players and almost instantly becoming best friends. This was despite being competitors fighting for the same position. We all shared the same interest and a common goal. As a group you have come together because of a shared passion and understanding of the level of stress and pressure you're under. It's special.

How did you both keep up with school during this time?
Adriana: That camp went for three days. We were in year ten at the time. Our school always supported us, even if we had to miss classes from time to time; however, we understood the importance of an education and never let our studies slip. I think our teachers appreciated that (our work ethic), so there was less concern if we had to skip classes.

We were organised and ensured we worked hard during the day at school, particularly if we had a long training session that night.

What were some of the challenges and feelings you experienced going into a more professional stage of your career?
Melissa: After the first camp, there were more camps and tournaments we attended. By this stage, we knew the players and how the camps worked, so the experience

PART 2: YOUTH DAYS

was less daunting; however, we started dealing with the sudden realisation there were new players coming in and others were no longer there. Positions were becoming more threatened. For example, there were three midfielders fighting for the same spot. You're trying to stay focused and trial to the best of your ability, but at the same time, the possibility of losing your spot is sitting in the back of your mind.

Adriana: You just have to do your best. That's all you can do. Go out there, perform to the best of your ability, have fun and see what happens.

Luckily for us, we were both chosen again, and as Young Matildas, we had to go to the AFC (Asian Football Confederation) Asian Cup qualifiers in Malaysia. This team was amazing! Some of our teammates were Clare Hunt, Ellie Carpenter and Alex Chidiac (all Matildas).

Melissa: It was such an emotional rollercoaster. I remember after our first training session, the coach called me over and said, *"You're not going to play in the midfield."* I instantly thought, *I'm the one. I'm the one that's not going to be picked for this team.* She then went on to say the midfield positions were filled, but she wanted me to play as a full back because she felt I was one of the better players and technically gifted.

I was torn between feeling like I wasn't good enough to play in the midfield but good enough to be wanted on the field. I wasn't sure how to take this or deal with it. There's a lot running through your mind. Emotions are up and down, but you must remain strong and take whatever you can get.

Adriana: I remember so clearly going into the changerooms for the first time and seeing my Matildas jersey hanging above my locker with my name on the back. That was an amazing feeling! Indescribable. Then you go out on the pitch, and you sing your country's national anthem. It was such an honour.

Melissa: Although we were seventeen years old, and it was with the Young Matildas, there are no words to explain how thrilling that moment was. It was the best feeling ever!

Adriana: We played Vietnam. I'm pretty sure I scored the first goal, and we won that game 7–0. We both played in the team again the next week and won that game too, but we lost the third game.

Mum and Dad came to watch us, but our older brother didn't as he was in a Melbourne City FC program at the time.

Seeing where some of your Young Matildas' teammates are now, is there any part of you that wishes you were there too?
Adriana: Those Matildas are amazing, and they deserve the success they have had. In the end, our experience turned out to be different. When we were with the Young Matildas, the coaches and senior management team said this is the most exciting group they'd ever seen and that they had all intentions of keeping the group together

for a long time.

We had to win or draw the last game in the Asian Cup qualifiers to make it through to the next round, but after we lost, we weren't sure if the coaches and senior management team felt the same. However, even after the loss, the bosses came in and reassured us they were happy with the level of talent this group had and that they still had intentions of keeping us together.

Unfortunately, once we got home, though, we didn't hear from them again, and we had to go about our normal life.

What did your normal life look like after the camp?
Adriana: It was really difficult going from life as a Young Matilda in the camp, where we would start our day off with a team walk, followed by a meal, and pre-game goal-setting and formation discussions, to getting up in the morning and going to English and maths classes. We would try to concentrate on school, wondering if we were going to get a call-up for the Young Matildas or Matildas' squad ever again. That period of waiting felt like torture, but that's just how it was and still is. You have to be patient in professional football, and you may or may not ever get that call.

Melissa: That was our first taste of what life as a professional football player was truly like.

What steps did or could you take in terms of your football career at this point?
Adriana: When we returned from the camp, we still played at NTC. Then we were asked to train with Melbourne Victory. This was when Joe Montemurro was the coach. He was a great coach and is a great person. He is now the coach of the Senior Women's Team at Juventus FC in Italy. I remember when I arrived at my first training session I didn't want to get out of the car. My legs felt like jelly, and I thought I had forgotten how to kick a ball.

Melissa: Despite the nerves, you just have to put one foot in front of the other and get out there.

Adriana: So that's what we did. I remember doing leg swings with one of the players who looked at me and blatantly asked me, *"Are you any good?"* I didn't know what to say, so I didn't say anything. Luckily, Joe Montemurro heard, so he responded with, *"Yes, they are, otherwise they wouldn't be here."* Hearing him say that helped me overcome some of the nerves and find the confidence to be on that training pitch and do my job.

I remember we did a drill whereby a defender had to go in and win the ball. One of the players asked how old we were. We were around sixteen years at the time, and when we told her, she said, *"Okay, so you're doing all the defending and running."* We thought she was joking, but she wasn't. We laugh about it now.

Melissa: We were the new young ones, so we did what we were told to do. We even had to pick up all the cones and collect all the balls after training. That's football, and funnily enough, it's one of the things we love about it. The camaraderie.

Everyone was so nice, and that was one of the best experiences of our lives. We got to train with some of the best players Australia has seen. It takes time to realise you belong with these great players, but slowly you become more and more confident and comfortable.

Adriana: We began as just players training with the Melbourne Victory team, then something amazing happened. Melbourne City FC was formed. Half of the Melbourne Victory players transferred to Melbourne City, so did the coach. We were both offered full-time professional contracts at Melbourne Victory and a full-time scholarship contract with Melbourne City at the same time. The difference is, with a full-time professional contract, you play games with the first team. With a scholarship contract, you just train with the first team. We had to decide. Do we sign with the club building a new team and offering to play us, or do we go with the team that has some of the greatest players in the world, and an amazing coach, but continue with just training? In terms of financial difference, back then it was $60 if you were on the bench and $100 if you got game time. It wasn't like it is now.

Melissa: We weren't naïve. We understood that while we were good players, Melbourne Victory also needed us to sign because they needed players at that time. We understood it was very unlikely we would've gotten a professional playing contract otherwise. It's important to think hard about decisions and make the most of the opportunities presented to you. These times can be difficult and confusing.

It's amazing being presented with such promising contracts, but you feel so stressed that you're going to make the wrong decision, which could jeopardise your career. It's moments like this you realise how important it is to have help and support from others. For us, it was our parents. They helped us weigh the different options, and they never forced us into doing what they wanted us to do or what they thought we should do. They allowed us to make the decisions we thought were right for us.

Adriana: With that being said, we chose to stay at Melbourne Victory. Like every player, we wanted to play. Were we ready? Probably not.

Joshua Risdon

"I believe this one decision, by one person who had faith in me, changed the course of my career. In my mind, it's the defining moment that led me to become what I had been desperately chasing my entire life, a professional football player."

Did you encounter any setbacks yourself during or around this stage of your football career?

Josh: At the end of the National Training Centre (NTC) and State season, we would go away with our U14 and U15 teams for a State competition. I was in the squad which was great, and we had a good State team, so we did really well. At this time, selections were being made for an U16–U17 national team called the Joeys. They were picking some of the U15s playing in the State carnival to be in this Australian team to go to an U17 World Cup.

Together with six of my State teammates, I made the shortlist, which consisted of approximately forty players; however, I and two of my teammates didn't make the final cut of twenty. I was told I was too small, not physically big enough, which is what selectors sometimes look for. I recall some of the players who got chosen were tall and developed.

How did you process that?

Josh: For me, the worst part about it was the person they chose for the right back position was a centre back player who was just bigger and stronger, not necessarily the greatest player. At the time, I felt like I deserved to be in that squad, so I was disappointed; however, I didn't let it affect me too much. I just kept going. I didn't want to hold a grudge, and to be honest, I don't think selectors spend too much time worrying about the feelings of the kids they don't pick. I would only be harming myself if I dropped my head and allowed my performance and goals to slip. I got back on the pitch, gave it my all and kept my head up.

You showed great resilience and persistence. Is that the key?

Josh: One hundred per cent. I think it's important to remind yourself (that) deselection is only one coach's opinion. That shouldn't change your mind or deter you from your goal. At some point, a new coach might come in and form a completely different opinion of the way you play and your performance. In the end, if it's what you want to do, it's

PART 2: YOUTH DAYS

important to continue to focus and not let someone's opinion, or any setback, deter you. It's okay to be dropped from the A team to the B team. Just keep going.

What did the rest of your youth days look like?
Josh: After my final year at NTC, there was another opportunity to get selected for the national team camp. Again, I worked hard. By this time, I was sixteen years old. The national team spoke to my NTC coach and asked him if he could play one of my teammates in the right back position instead of me because they were looking at selecting him for the Australian squad. The player they were interested in usually played in the right-wing position, and I remember him being extremely fast and physical.

As a result, I was dropped from the NTC first eleven, and I sat on the bench for the last four or five games of the season. It was the first time I experienced sitting on the bench for full games, and it was hard for me to fathom. I remember my mum and dad driving up to watch me play, and all they got to see was me sitting, which made me feel bad for them.

Despite that, I knew this decision was out of my coach's control, and to give him due credit, he did provide me with an explanation. With that said, the reason became obvious.

How were you feeling at that point?
Josh: At this point, I started thinking, *Where does this leave me now?*

How did you approach training and games after experiencing this?
Josh: After this happened, there were times when I would question the point of it all. I often wondered if I would ever get another chance, but I went back to training and pushed on.

There are times you will feel upset, particularly when you experience these kinds of setbacks, but you're only doing yourself harm if you don't strive to become a better player. I chose to turn up, be happy and contribute to my team in any way I could.

At what point did you start to think about a backup plan in case football didn't work out?
Josh: I left school in year eleven because the financial burden on my parents to continue paying for an apartment in Perth weighed on me. I wanted to get a job and try to pay my own way. I didn't know what I wanted to do, but I decided on a Certificate in Commercial Cooking. I began working as a trainee at a restaurant called Sizzlers. I don't remember if I actively thought about it, but perhaps it was my mind's way of telling me this could be an option if football doesn't work out. I was sixteen years old, coming out of the NTC and wondering what was next for me.

Why cooking?
Josh: I lived by myself from the age of fourteen, so I had to learn how to cook from a young age, and I didn't mind cooking.

What did your daily life look like?
Josh: I would go to work, then go straight to training. They were long days. On weekends, I wanted to go out with school friends, but I rarely did because I had games on the weekend, and my parents were still coming up to visit. I wanted to spend my time with them when I could.

How did that impact your relationships with your school friends?
Josh: The relationships I made at school in Perth became a bit distant because I wasn't going out with them on weekends and doing what other normal sixteen-year-olds were.

Do you feel like you missed out on a little bit of your childhood?
Josh: Yes. I had fun experiences throughout high school and still hold on to some fond memories, but I did miss out on a lot. In fact, I don't have a close group of lifelong mates, the kind of friendships you generally form in high school, because I was always at football. It probably didn't help (that) I left school in year eleven.

Getting back to football, where did you go after NTC finished?
Josh: I went back to my old club ECU Joondalup and started playing in the first team. We were playing in the highest league in Perth.

That's quite an achievement. How did that feel for you?
Josh: It was a good feeling, getting into and being part of this squad at such a young age.

This was my first experience of being paid to play too. It wasn't much, but it was still a positive step for me.

You were playing in the first team at ECU Joondalup. Where did you go from there?
Josh: It was while I was playing with this team that I started to develop an interest in trying out for an A-League Youth Team. I set my sights on that. It became my next goal; however, halfway through my first season with ECU Joondalup, I broke my ankle. The break happened right before the commencement of the A-League Youth Team trials. I thought my chance of making the youth team had become non-existent. I wasn't going to be fit to play again until a couple of games into the season, and who would want to select a player in this predicament?

This was hard for me because I genuinely thought I had a chance of getting in. I knew they were looking at players who had come from NTC, and I was playing well.

PART 2: YOUTH DAYS

I felt like I ticked all the right boxes. The coach of the A-League Youth Team at the time had also been my U13 State team coach, so he knew my capabilities and level of dedication.

Despite my ankle, I went to the trials on my crutches and watched the team train from behind the fence on the sidelines. I didn't think I had any chance of being selected, but in the only way I could, I wanted to show them I was keen and committed despite my current circumstances.

It paid off because the coach took a chance on me and offered me a contract. I believe this one decision, by one person who had faith in me, changed the course of my career. In my mind, it's the defining moment that led me to become what I had been desperately chasing my entire life, a professional football player.

The contract was for a scholarship, and the coach told me he didn't want me to worry about the trials and wanted me to simply focus on getting better.

I will be forever grateful to this coach.

When did you return to playing, and what was that like?
Josh: I missed the first few games, but it wasn't long before I came back fit and played in the youth team. We had a great team that year and made the Grand Final. We lost, but I did well. I played most of the games. The only time I didn't play was when players from the first team came down and stepped in. Being a first-team player, they are understandably always given priority.

I was seventeen, and I had also moved out and started living with my sister, who had moved to Perth.

What was it like living with your sister?
Josh: It was unreal! I loved living with her. To be honest, I was a bit nervous to start with because I hadn't seen her much growing up. She is a lot older than me, and I moved away at such a young age, but it turned out to be amazing. The best! It was so nice being with my family again every day. This was something I had missed so much. My sister and I have this strong connection now, which I attribute to the time we had together.

MAKING IT...OR NOT

Chloe Logarzo

"Despite all those times I wasn't selected and others were, it turned out I ended up 'making it' and a lot of them didn't. That is why it's important to keep pushing through the tough times."

How did your youth days start out?
Chloe: After finally making it onto the New South Wales team, my coach invited me to train with Sydney FC. I jumped at the opportunity, and one day was offered a chance because one of the girls on the team tore her ACL (anterior cruciate ligament). I got what they called an 'Injury Contract'. I didn't have any expectations of playing though.

Did you have to give up or sacrifice other things to take on this new role?
Chloe: By this stage, I had to give up playing with my representative club because I was playing for New South Wales Institute of Sport (NSWIS) as well.

How had your training schedule changed?
Chloe: I was sixteen years old and began training five nights a week and on Friday mornings. The load and expectations had increased tremendously from my younger days.

How did you keep up with other things during this time, including homework?
Chloe: It was hard, but I had to make it work. I did year twelve over two years because I had missed too many classes to attend football commitments. I was nineteen when I graduated from high school.

How did you manage the logistics of getting to school, then to football training?
Chloe: I still lived at home, so my mum or dad would wake up at five o'clock in the morning every Friday to take me to training, which started at six o'clock, then I would go to school straight from training. You can't underestimate how much parents do and sacrifice. If they aren't committed to you 'making it', then it is very hard for you to do that. I know of one girl whose parents would drive three hours to training and three hours back, which is incredible. Parental support is imperative.

When did you become part of the Young Matildas?
Chloe: At eighteen, I was given my first opportunity to make the Youth National Team camp, or the Young Matildas' squad. I made that team and toured with them

PART 2: YOUTH DAYS

for two years before I became too old to continue.

What was it like being a Young Matilda?
Chloe: I was eighteen and nineteen years old when I travelled with my teammates. I was having so much fun I didn't care too much about whether I played or not. I was simply grateful to be there and embraced the opportunity.

The team went to New Zealand and Myanmar in Asia to play a qualifier. It was a great experience. I was one of the older players, and I was made captain. I felt honoured, especially after all the setbacks I had experienced earlier in my football journey. Representing my country was an honour I didn't take for granted.

These days, it's different. I believe the Young Matildas care more about playing and winning because the name 'Matilda' holds more weight now. When I was a Young Matilda, it wasn't a big name.

During this time, did you witness others get deselected or injured?
Chloe: It's funny because there might only be four or five of us left, of all the girls who were selected for the youth New South Wales teams and the Young Matildas. Despite the times I wasn't selected, and others were, it turned out I ended up 'making it', and a lot of them didn't. That is why it's important to keep pushing through the tough times.

I could name fifteen players that aren't even involved in football anymore.

Did you witness devastation?
Chloe: Not really because, at that time, you had to decide whether you were going to choose to make money in a traditional career and have a social life or if you were going to tough it out with no money and try to 'make it'.

At what age did you start playing with the Sydney FC first team?
Chloe: I was sixteen or seventeen years old when I had my debut with Sydney FC. It took someone to get injured for me to have my chance. The only other way I could've been picked was to be better than the other players, but that was very difficult because it was a very 'stacked era'.

What do you mean by a 'stacked era'?
Chloe: There were a lot of Matildas on the team, including Caitlyn Foord, Samantha Kerr and Kyah Simon, to name a few. At that time, the Matilda Team consisted of players mostly from Sydney FC and Brisbane Roar.

As the new kid, I never expected an opportunity to play because there were so many girls on my team older and more experienced than I was. I was just a kid grateful to be there.

When did you leave to pursue your career in America?
Chloe: I went overseas after high school to play in the second division in America.

There was an Australian coach over there who called me and told me it would be a great opportunity. I wanted to go overseas anyway, but I hadn't been playing enough to be able to go straight to a club and get paid, so I left my family for the first time and lived with a host family in Colorado, USA as an amateur in the second division. I was there for five months with no pay.

How did you feel about leaving your family for the first time?
Chloe: I felt this sense of freedom and believed this was the perfect opportunity for me to experience what it was like to pursue football as a career.

What was your season like in America?
Chloe: I had an unbelievable season! I scored the most goals ever, had the most assists, was a regular in the starting eleven, was awarded one of the 'Best Eleven', and was named 'Best Player'.

When did you return home, and what happened then?
Chloe: After my season in America, I went back to Sydney FC. The coach had big expectations of me because I had done so well overseas. By this time, I had also made it into the Matildas national team squad. I was twenty years old. Unfortunately, I had become 'bigheaded', so I only played three games in my first season back at Sydney FC. My attitude was terrible. I got too big for my own boots, so the coach rightfully benched me. He had coached me from the age of twelve, so he witnessed the shift in my attitude. He taught me the valuable lesson of remaining humble and down to earth, probably one of the most important life lessons you can have.

I didn't have a great season that year, but I pushed on and stayed at Sydney FC for a couple more seasons. I focused on getting better and tried to earn my spot in the first eleven again.

Can you explain your debut and time with the Matildas?
Chloe: I debuted with the Matildas in a game against China. I didn't expect to be asked to go, but once again, someone got injured, so I was called up to attend the camp. The first camp the coach brought me to, I debuted straight away. I played my first few minutes with the national team, felt amazing and was thinking, *This is great!* The coach then took the team to Cyprus for a tournament. We didn't do well there, but I played a couple of games. I was in and out of the national team at this time. It wasn't like I was a regular, nor was I being asked to attend every camp.

I hadn't cemented my spot yet. Soon, the Matildas got a new coach.

PART 2: YOUTH DAYS

Were you nervous about this?
Chloe: I was quite nervous about who was going to come in, but when I found out who that was, I became excited because he watched me grow up as a player. He knew what sort of player I was and understood my work ethic.

Did you progress as a Matilda under his management?
Chloe: When he became the national team coach, I felt like I slowly started to cement my spot on the team. This is why, when he didn't select me for the 2015 FIFA World Cup, I was devastated. So devastated I went off the rails.

What did 'going off the rails' look like for you?
Chloe: I was so upset that I did what I thought was rational at the time: I quit football. I resented football for taking a normal life away from me. Being a professional footballer means making a lot of sacrifices. I sacrificed a normal, young-adult life, consisting of going out with friends and going on holidays. I didn't do any of the fun and exciting things everyone else at that age did. I felt robbed of those years of my life because I dedicated them to playing football. I put all my eggs in one basket, so when I was told I wasn't going to go do something I had worked so hard for, I was devastated.

I started working as a landscaper six to seven days a week. I saved up as much money as I could, and I travelled for two months. I went to the Philippines, Greece, Croatia, Malta and Italy. I didn't play any football. I went to a lot of parties. I wanted to do everything I felt I missed out on in the five years I chased my football dream.

I remember being in a bar in Greece watching the women's World Cup and thinking, *That could've been me.* By the time I reached Italy, my last destination, it really hit me. The tears came with a vengeance. I cried so much. Eventually, I picked myself up and decided I was going to go home, and instead of playing for Sydney FC, I wanted to try and play for Newcastle United. I decided on Newcastle United because the team is based in New South Wales where my family is, and I wanted to be close to home.

Before I could even think about that, I knew I had to get my fitness back, so I started running in Italy. I couldn't even run five hundred metres without struggling, so I crouched down and, again, started crying profusely. I couldn't believe the position I had put myself in. Deep down it was clear I still wanted to be a footballer.

Looking back, do you think there were any positives in taking this break?
Chloe: I'm grateful for the experiences I had while travelling and for taking the time to see what it's like to have a 'normal' job. Stepping away for a while allowed me to rekindle my love for football again.

So, what happened when you returned home from your travels?
Chloe: I went to Newcastle United. The coach, Craig Deans, 'Deansy', believed in me. He felt I had the potential to get back into the Matildas. He promised to work with me as much as he could, and he did.

Did you get back into the Matildas' squad?
Chloe: It was 2016 and the World Cup had just ended, so the next thing was the Olympic qualifiers.

Obviously, I hadn't been on the national team for a while, and I went back to landscaping. I had to earn money because the most I was getting paid from football was $4,000 to $5,000 per year. That wasn't even enough to cover petrol to and from training. My landscaping boss was my old assistant coach at Sydney FC, so he understood the need for flexibility and arranged for me to, at the very least, be able to train with the Matildas when they needed an extra player.

While the Matildas were at the Australian Institute of Sport (AIS) for camp, I was in Canberra working at a retirement village as a landscaper. I would wear my high vis uniform and work boots to lay pavers in the morning from six o'clock to ten o'clock, then the Matildas would train from eleven o'clock to two o'clock. I would drive from where I was working to the AIS, arrive in my work clothes, change into a pair of borrowed boots, throw on a Matildas jersey, and play training matches. Afterwards, I would go back to my landscaping job and do that until 6 p.m. I did that for days on end, until I was selected to attend the next Matildas' camp for the Tokyo Olympic qualifiers.

Did you go to the Tokyo Olympics, and if so, what was that experience like?
Chloe: I hadn't played with the national team in a long time, and there I was in Tokyo. I couldn't believe it! I played the best I had ever played in my entire life at those qualifiers. I played every single minute of every single game. We qualified for the Olympics, for the first time in twelve years, which was special. That tournament solidified my spot in the Matildas' squad. From then on, unless injured, I was in the starting eleven for every game, which continued for the next four years.

So, you became an Olympian. Where did you go after the Games came to an end?
Chloe: Yes, I became an Olympian! It was after that campaign I signed my first professional contract with Swedish club Eskilstuna United. That club was great.

PART 2: YOUTH DAYS

Emily Gielnik

"I remember turning up the following day, feeling incredibly nervous and scared, thinking to myself, This is my shot, and I have two options. I can either let this make or break me. I'm either going to sink or swim. *I ended up having the best session of my life."*

At what point did you return to football outside of school?
Emily: The school football teams went on a field trip to the Australian Institute of Sport (AIS) in Canberra one day. The Matildas happened to be training there on that day, and my teacher came up to me and said, *"I hope you don't mind, but I'm going to ask the Matildas coach if you can train with them."* I thought, *What?* I was just a girl on a school excursion.

What happened?
Emily: I was convinced they would say no, but my school coach came back to me and said, *"You're training with them tomorrow, and by the way, it's a conditioning session, so it's going to be tough."* I remember feeling shocked and then petrified.

I remember turning up the following day, feeling incredibly nervous and scared, thinking to myself, *This is my shot, and I have two options. I can either let this make or break me. I'm either going to sink or swim.* I ended up having the best session of my life. I was fifteen years old.

How did the other players treat you?
Emily: They were nice to me. They didn't take it easy on me though, and during training, it was 'go time'. Overall, it was an amazing experience. I had never felt so exhausted, but I was in fight-or-flight mode, and I chose to fight.

The Matildas coach then approached my school coach and told him the Matildas were playing against a boys team the following day, and he wanted me to play with them. I remember thinking, *What? Am I hearing right?* I couldn't believe what I heard, particularly after so many years of not getting selected. Here I was, having skipped all the 'normal' steps most players have to take to get into a national team, and I was getting a call back after being on a random school trip. It was so bizarre! I remember thinking, there is no way the coach would allow me to put on a yellow Matildas jersey if he didn't think I was good enough. That's when my confidence reignited for the first time in a long time.

What was that game like for you?

Emily: My whole school team came and watched me play. I was very nervous, but despite that, I played well. The next day the Matildas coach rang the head coach of the QAS program and told him he met this girl who had to be in the QAS program. That was how I eventually got into the QAS program.

Now, I'm back with all my friends who had initially gotten into the QAS program when I had been denied the opportunity, then over the course of the next couple of years, some of those players started to drop off, and I began to surpass them.

Do you think that in the end, 'making it' comes down to mental stamina?

Emily: Absolutely! Perseverance and resilience are essential. You need to have that burning desire to be there. I believe there are two types of people in this world: those who are told 'no' and accept it, and those who are told 'no' and do something about it. What I still suffer from to this day, though, is the need for someone to believe in me, and I attribute that to my challenging start in football as a junior.

PART 2: YOUTH DAYS

Callum Nicholas

"I remember later that day seeing it on Instagram with a caption that read 'Cal Nic on Lallana at a training session.' It had 100,000 likes, and I thought, What? *That was the moment it hit me that I had just trained with the Liverpool first team."*

Did you get offered a scholarship with Manchester United?
Callum: I was doing really well at United, even in my U16 year. Everyone thought I was guaranteed a scholarship; however, we had a tournament in Slovakia, and every player getting a scholarship was going, but when I looked at the sheet, my name wasn't on it. I was shocked and couldn't understand why. I remember my dad rang one of the coaches and told them if I wasn't going to get a contract, they needed to tell me. The same day, my dad and I got called into the office. I was in the physio room because I had an injury. When I arrived, they told me I wasn't getting a scholarship. My dad was fuming because he believed I deserved it.

Did you ever find out why you weren't offered a scholarship?
Callum: I don't believe it was about technical ability or performance. The year above me had a certain number of midfielders, and in my age group, they took six players. One player had been injured for three years, but they recalled him being good from when he was younger. I think they decided to take a risk on him as opposed to me. Funnily enough, when it was time for him to start the scholarship, he decided not to pursue it. He didn't enjoy it so called it quits.

How did you feel?
Callum: I was gutted. I had been with the club for many years, and I was committed. It felt like home for me. If I didn't think I was good enough, or hadn't done well, I would've dealt with the setback a bit better, perhaps looked for a club in a lower league, but that wasn't the case. Everyone expected me to get a scholarship, which made it even harder to understand.

I also felt like I had let my dad down a little bit. He put so much effort into taking me to each session for years.

Did your dad ever push you?
Callum: He did a little bit when I was a kid. To be honest, I used to prefer when my mum took me to my games because she wouldn't say anything [*Callum laughs*].

Sometimes, the car ride home was interesting. My mum and dad sometimes got into an argument because my dad would want me to know what I did wrong, whereas my mum would tell him to leave me alone. My dad was my biggest fan, and when I did well, his reaction was amazing.

I remember one day, when I reached a turning point and started to perform well, around fourteen or fifteen years old, I got into the car after my match, and my dad shook my hand and said, *"Wow, you were awesome!"* That motivated me to keep pushing and getting better.

What did you do after Manchester United didn't offer you a scholarship?
Callum: I looked for another club as my name was listed on an online platform other clubs and agents have access to. At sixteen, I got an agent too. Before then, I didn't have one, because I assumed I wasn't going to need one, but a few of us who got released talked, and I received a recommendation from another player.

My new agent received several phone calls from different clubs when I was released. I received offers from West Bromwich Albion, Leicester, Liverpool, Tottenham, Leeds, Blackburn, Reading and South Hampton. Some of them wanted me to attend a trial, while others offered me a contract without having to trial. I wanted the best deal I could get that would give me a pathway to a professional contract.

One of the decisions I regret now was one I made when I was sixteen. West Bromwich Albion FC offered me a one-year scholarship followed by a two-year professional contract, and I didn't take it.

I remember going on trial at Leicester. They wanted to offer me a scholarship. I went to Tottenham too. They wanted to sign me as well. Leeds offered me a one-year scholarship and three-year professional contract. At the Leeds trial, I was sixteen and training with the U23 squad. I remember stalling on their offer because I knew Liverpool and Tottenham were interested too, and they were the clubs that attracted me the most.

I thought to myself that if I'm good enough, I'll get a professional contract regardless. My agent warned me it didn't work like that, and I could end up with an injury or another setback, which turned out to be the case.

I went to Tottenham and knew they wanted to sign me, but as soon as I came back from my Tottenham trial, I went to Liverpool. I remember the coach was Michael Beale. He's the coach at Rangers now. He's a good coach, and he couldn't believe it when he saw me walk in. He remembered me from when his team played against mine at Manchester United. He knew I was a good player, so he started questioning why Manchester United let me go. He wondered if there was another reason, like my attitude or personality. He rang United to find out, and United confirmed there was no issue with me as a person. The reason was they had too many kids

PART 2: YOUTH DAYS

and couldn't fit me into their program.

You had to make a tough decision. What did your dad think?
Callum: My dad agreed with me. He thought that if I went to one of the best clubs, then I was going to have to be one of the best to get a contract. I preferred this because it made me work harder.

So how important is it for players, and even parents, to maintain the right attitude?
Callum: Very important. Clubs often won't choose players because of bad behaviour or attitude, and the word can spread from club to club. The same applies if parents are difficult.

What happened following your trial with Liverpool?
Callum: I did well at my trial with Liverpool, and they offered me a scholarship. There was no guarantee of a professional contract though. I know I had better offers from other clubs, and my agent at the time wanted me to take the Leeds offer because it was the longest contract, but when I was at Liverpool, I felt like it was the right fit for me. Logistically it wasn't too far from home either.

How far was it from where you were living at that time?
Callum: It was a forty-minute drive.

Who were you living with?
Callum: I lived with a woman who looked after me and another player from Manchester United, Cameron Brannagan. He helped look after me as well. He was a few years older than me and was in the first team. In fact, he eventually went on to play in the Champions League with Liverpool.

How old were you at this time?
Callum: I was sixteen years old.

How did you find moving away from home?
Callum: I hated it! I wasn't driving, so I would have to rely on my dad to pick me up on the weekends to take me home to be with my family. On a Sunday night, he would drive me back, and sometimes, I would get really upset knowing I was going to be away from my family for another week. I remember one time I started crying in the car, and my dad asked me what was wrong. I told him I didn't enjoy living away from home. Having no licence meant I couldn't see friends or family whenever I wanted. My life was just football.

How did you get to training during the week then?
Callum: The club would pick us up.

Did you start to feel a bit better once you got your licence?
Callum: As soon as I started driving, it was a lot better, and I didn't mind living away from home as much.

At what age can you get your licence in the UK?
Callum: You can start driving at seventeen, but I was eighteen by the time I got my licence because I failed my driving test a few times [*Callum laughs*].

Why? What happened?
Callum: I went for my licence test in Liverpool. The first time, I accidentally pulled out onto a roundabout when I shouldn't have, so I didn't get my licence then. The second time, I went for my test straight after training, so I was in my Liverpool tracksuit. The driving instructor was a big Everton supporter. I genuinely believe he failed me because I played for Liverpool. The third time, my confidence was a bit broken, so I failed because I drove too slowly. The fourth time, I decided to go for my licence in Manchester. I passed that one.

Going back to football, what happened after you signed at Liverpool?
Callum: Once you pass U16, you become a full-time footballer and you start fighting for a position in the U18 team. I was one of the younger players, and the older players in the U18 Liverpool squad at that time were among the most talented in England. Many of those players ended up in the first team and are playing in the Premier League now. Three or four younger players were asked to play every week in this team, and I was lucky enough to have been one of them.

Did you struggle for game time, or if not, did you see others struggle?
Callum: I didn't struggle for game time, but yes, I did see others struggle. Some players didn't play all year.

As a full-time footballer at this time, what was your income like?
Callum: Some of my teammates, the ones with a professional contract, were on around 10,000 pounds a week. As someone on a scholarship, I wasn't even getting 200 pounds per week. Despite that, I got game time, sometimes out of my usual position, but I didn't care. As long as I was playing, I was happy.

PART 2: YOUTH DAYS

Did you play against your old club Manchester United?
Callum: Yes. I remember the first time I played against United. It was live on TV. Marcus Rashford and Scott McTominay played then and still do now. They had a very good team. Both Marcus and I were on the bench to start with because we were the younger players at the time. Liverpool was winning 3-0 then I came on at half-time because one of my teammates got injured. I played really well, and we won that game 4-0.

How was the rest of that season for you?
Callum: I played quite well that season, even scored a few goals. I wasn't in the starting lineup every week, but I often came on halfway through the games. Just to be selected, to be part of this team each week, was a good outcome for my age.

If the U23 squad had a game, the first team would choose some players from our U18 team to go up and train with the first team. I was seventeen when I was asked to train with the first team for the first time.

Wow. How were you asked?
Callum: My name was just listed on a WhatsApp group.

How did that first training session feel with the Liverpool first team?
Callum: I remember being in the changeroom before we went out, wondering who was going to be there. The thing I remember the most was the smell. There was such a strong smell of aftershave [*Callum laughs*].

We went out, and Brendan Rogers, who was the coach at the time, explained to us what we were going to do during training. We started with a lap around the pitch, and I ran alongside Steven Gerrard who was the team captain. He asked, *"Where you from, lad?"* I replied, *"Manchester."* He then joked, *"Why do we keep signing lads from Manchester?"* We laughed. He made me feel very welcome.

We went on to play a game in small groups. I remember thinking that Adam Lallana is the best player by far, but as soon as we joined together and started playing on a bigger pitch, Steven Gerrard blew my mind. He was so good!

The thing about that training session was less mistakes. No one really makes a mistake.

Did you feel added pressure because of this?
Callum: No. I really enjoyed it. When you get the ball, you don't want to look stupid, so you play it simple. You avoid taking risks, but you should, to stand out a bit more.

Did anything else happen that made this moment so memorable?
Callum: After that training session with the Liverpool first team, I waited for my driver to pick me up, and I saw the photographer. I asked him if he had taken any good photos. He showed me some that he took of me and asked if I wanted him to put them on Liverpool's Instagram page. I didn't say no to that.

I remember seeing it on Instagram later that day with a caption that read *'Cal Nic on Lallana at a training session.'* It had 100,000 likes, and I thought *What?* That was the moment it hit me that I had just trained with the Liverpool first team.

My dad recorded the session off the Liverpool TV channel, then he posted that footage on Instagram as well. It was a proud moment.

How many times did you get invited to join the first team for training?
Callum: In my first year, it was probably four or five times.

One day, they asked a few of us to go to a behind-closed-doors friendly game against the Wolves (Wolverhampton Wanderers). I started on the bench but ended up being substituted on for the last ten minutes of the game in the midfield next to Steven Gerrard. It was a pinch-me moment.

That day was the first time Trent Alexander-Arnold played with the first team as well.

Trent Alexander-Arnold has gone on to have quite the successful career. In fact, I remember Steven Gerrard was writing a book at the time, and he said in his book that Trent would be the next star player. He was right.

PART 2: YOUTH DAYS

Diogo Ferreira

"It was harder each time I would leave after coming back home for a holiday. I would go out with friends and really enjoy my life. It's important to have a balance and still enjoy your life."

What made you think *I'm ready for Porto*?
Diogo: When I was twelve years old, I went with my family on a holiday to Portugal. While there, I trained with a competitive team. They wanted me to stay, but at that time my parents said no. Knowing this, my passion for the sport grew. I began to think maybe I was good enough to pursue football as a career, and it gave me the drive to want to go back one day.

How did you get to Porto given you were so young?
Diogo: I made the move to Porto FC when I was fifteen years old. I have to say this is where people sometimes get it wrong. My dad was involved in football back then, so some people thought I went because of my dad. Did my dad help me get a trial through someone he knew? Yes, 100 per cent, but then it was up to me. Knowing someone helps, maybe that's where luck comes into it, but it's still up to each kid to perform, especially overseas where it's harder to get recognised.

There's no room for parents to sponsor clubs and offer thousands of dollars to get their child in. These are big clubs. These clubs invest their time and money in players from a young age. They are a serious business.

What was it like leaving your family to go to Portugal at the age of fifteen?
Diogo: I think it was harder for my parents than it was for me, especially my mum. The whole idea of going to Porto was driven by me. My parents didn't want me to go, but they saw it was my dream. It's all I ever spoke about, and I worked hard at my game. They saw this, so they supported me. Thankfully, I was mature enough by this age.

My parents tell a story about a friend of theirs who told them that if your son walks through the departure gates at the airport and looks back at you, he won't last. Apparently, I didn't look back. Was I sad? Of course, I was; I love my family. Did I cry? No, I didn't. No one was forcing me to go, so I didn't feel the need to cry.

It was harder each time I would leave after coming back home for a holiday. I would go out with friends and really enjoy my life. It's important to have a balance and still enjoy your life. However, as hard as it was, I would still go back to Portugal because a professional football career was ultimately what I wanted.

I stayed in Portugal for three years.

What were your living arrangements like?
Diogo: I was in a house with kids from other parts of Europe, including Portugal, where it was too far for them to travel. We were given a roof over our heads; breakfast, lunch and dinner; and someone to look after us. If the club sees something in you, they will let you stay, but if they don't, you're released.

What did a day in the life at Porto look like for you?
Diogo: I got up in the morning and went to school. I would come home and have lunch, then in the afternoon, a bus would pick me and the others up and take us to training. We would then come home from training, have dinner and go to sleep. That was our life.

What was school like?
Diogo: When I first went to Portugal, I went to a Portuguese-speaking school. I was in year ten in Australia and went into year eight there. I can speak Portuguese, but I still found it difficult. Eventually, I found distance education, which was unheard of twenty years ago when I went overseas. You could do distance education if you were an athlete representing your country or pursuing sport at a high level, so I fit the criteria. That's how I chose to continue my education. I would stay home on my laptop while everyone else went to school. My mum helped me a lot with my homework.

What was your experience like as a player for Porto?
Diogo: I was confident enough to feel I belonged, and I got so much better while I was there. By the end, I was playing games, and everything seemed to be going well; however, the year after, Porto wanted to keep me but loan me out.

I knew there were players who were better than me, and I had a long way to go. I was realistic. I knew my limitations and level of ability. I knew I wasn't going to get playing time. Staying at Porto just for the sake of it was not going to work for me. I decided it was best for me to stay in Portugal but go to a smaller club, so I went to AD Oeiras. I still played in the same league as Porto, Benfica, Sporting, etc., and two seasons later we finished on top of them in my age group. We had a good team, and I was captain. It was fantastic!

How did you feel when you found out Porto wanted to loan you out?
Diogo: I was upset, but even at such a young age, I was realistic. I remember my dad saying to me that if they wanted me to stay, then maybe I should just stay. I didn't

want that because I knew I wasn't at the level required, and looking back, I feel I made the best decision. I played in the same league, and I played every week. That made me happy.

This reminds me, parents these days need to consider whether they want their children to play on the B team and be on the pitch or on the A team but only play for ten minutes. If a child is not playing, that kid is not developing.

What were some challenges you experienced while living in Portugal?
Diogo: I'm the kind of person who doesn't complain much, but a support network was still necessary. I used to speak to my parents every day, and apparently, whatever I felt would dictate their feelings for that day too. I found this out later when I came home.

I remember being bullied by one of the kids in the house I lived in. My impression was the kids in Portugal live a much tougher life. They are very mature for their age, and being successful in their career feels like 'life or death' to them. I remember one of the players on my team telling me once that if he didn't make it in football, he would go to jail. When I asked him what he meant by that, he replied, *"Because if I go to jail at least I will get food each day."*

My family wasn't rich, but they would buy me nice things from time to time. I felt like I had to hide them, otherwise I wouldn't fit in or feel accepted. It was hard to be my true self.

I also had to be mindful that for me to sign with Porto would inevitably mean another player living in the house was dropped. I had players approach me and demand, *"Get out. We lost him because of you."* I was taken aback by this but persisted by maintaining a low profile and working hard at training and during games. In the end, I gained their respect, and I became mates with all of them.

Callum Nicholas with his family after signing his first contract with Manchester United

Callum Nicholas in action with semi-professional club Prestwich Heys AFC in Manchester, England

Celebrating a win with semi-professional club, FC Strathmore Splits, in Melbourne, Australia

Chloe Logarzo training with Washington Spirit

Chloe Logarzo acknowledging Sydney FC fans post-game while using a crutch to aid an injury

A young Diogo Ferreira with Portuguese superstar Joao Pinto

Diogo Ferreira coaching at his DF Football Academy

Diogo Ferreira warming up the Australian U23 squad

Diogo played with Brisbane Roar in their 2014 premiership season

Emily Gielnick with Bayern Munich FC

Emily Gielnik in action with Melbourne Victory FC

Emily Gielnik (#15) with the Matildas celebrating a goal with Chloe Logarzo (#6) and Sam Kerr (#20)

Josh Risdon as a junior

Josh Risdon playing in the Youth Championships in Western Australia

Josh Risdon representing the Socceroos

Josh Risdon in action vs England at the Stadium of Light, Sunderland, May 2016

Adriana and Melissa Taranto representing the young Matildas

Adriana and Melissa Taranto with Western United

Melissa Taranto after she scored in the 80th minute to put her team into the Nike Cup final, which they went on to win.

Part 3:
Going Pro

This is the real journey, where you see what it takes to go pro.

The sacrifices made and pressures felt by a professional footballer can be tremendous. Mental toughness is incredibly important, more so than technical skill. It's one thing to get there; it's another to stay.

The players in this book provide important lessons on managing this period of a football career. Some paused to rekindle their love for the game; some will teach us how to recover from emotional and physical challenges. They all demonstrate a high level of resilience. By reading their stories, you'll realise the road to the top is never easy or a straight line, and patience is key.

Pro Stats

- Less than 1 per cent of players will be offered a professional contract. To put this into perspective, out of 1,000 players, less than 10 will ever go pro.
- Going pro in soccer is all about having emotional resilience, more so than what you can do with your feet.
- 'Youth players at an English Premier League academy, who eventually went pro, showed mental toughness from a young age. These players had a commitment to learning, a strong level of trust in their coach, were compliant in instruction, and were always looking for ways to improve' —*Science Daily,* University of Lincoln, June 19, 2014.

MAKING IT...OR NOT

Melissa and Adriana Taranto

*"Sometimes you need to take a step back,
rebuild your confidence, surround
yourself with the right people and immerse yourself
in the right culture to rise again."*

What did your day-to-day lives look like during your time with Melbourne Victory?
Melissa: We lived on one side of town and Melbourne Victory trained on the other side of town. It often took us two hours to get there, particularly during peak traffic time. By then, we were in year twelve and each doing one university subject, which meant we didn't finish school until 4:30 p.m. We would run home after school, dump our school stuff, get changed into our football kits, and hop into the car with dinner Dad had pre-made and put into containers for us. Dad would drive us in heavy traffic to training ... and this was a man who also worked night shifts at the time. Mum and Dad often shared this load. Without our parents, we would never have been able to do it. The sacrifices they made were huge.

Adriana: Dad would sit in the car and wait for us while we trained for an hour and a half. Unfortunately, I remember going through a period around this time when I began to hate football. I felt like we were thrown in to play in the highest league in Australia, and we weren't ready. I put a lot of pressure on myself during this time too. For example, if I took one bad touch at training, I would have nightmares about that.

Melissa: I was more frustrated with the amount of travelling required. It was exhausting, and we felt it.

Adriana: On top of that, we were told as a group at the last training session of each week who would be in the starting eleven on the weekend. This was an intense moment each time. Everyone would have their head down pretending to be stretching, anxiously waiting for their name to be called. Away games were bittersweet. The worst thing about it was if you weren't selected for the team when playing away, it meant you couldn't travel with the team. Travelling was sometimes the best part. Our first game of the season was away, and I remember my sister got picked and I didn't. My heart fell to the floor, and I had to fight back tears. I got in the car, let it out and continually asked myself *"Why?"*

PART 3: GOING PRO

Melissa: This is the difference between the junior years, which should be fun, and the youth and professional years. There's often a noticeable gap in talent when you're young, in your junior days. As you get older, that gap closes, so the competition becomes greater and fiercer.

How did you find joy again when you were going through difficult times?
Adriana: We were brought up to believe that if someone tells you you're not good enough, use that to motivate you to prove them wrong. I dealt with my setback by taking a couple of days to be emotional and question why, but then picked myself up again, turned up to training with a positive attitude, and did my best to help my team. I went in hard, encouraged my teammates, and helped prepare them for the game ahead. That was my purpose during those weeks. You have to have this mentality if you want to 'make it'.

I also had to put on a brave face to be there for my sister.
Melissa: I remember we didn't win that game, but it was such a big learning experience for us as a team. Sometimes, not being in the best team and playing against much tougher teams helps you become a better player. I remember playing against Kim Little and Jess Fishlock in that first game against Melbourne City. Our team barely touched the ball.

Adriana: My first game ended up being at Hume Stadium against Perth Glory. I went on in the 75th minute, and I played against Sam Kerr. I remember freaking out and thinking, What am I doing here? I don't think I touched the ball. I could barely breathe. That was my debut into the Women's A-League. It was very challenging; however, it was good because it got easier for me after that.

I think after that, we both became regular starting eleven players.
Melissa: I remember we often had conversations with each other about trying to find the fun in what we were doing again, because when you reach that level, it can often be less enjoyable. The nerves, the pressure, the self-doubt and being your own worst critic can take away the joy.

How long were you both with your first professional club?
Adriana: We continued to play at Melbourne Victory for another season, and for the first time ever, we were substituting for each other on game day. We didn't understand this because we always felt we played better together and were more of an asset to the team when we were both on the pitch at the same time. We had strong chemistry because we knew each other's style of play.

Did you feel comfortable asking the coach if you weren't sure about decisions?
Melissa: It was important by this stage to treat each other as two separate professional individuals, so we would never approach the coach about why we both weren't on the pitch at the same time. However, if I wasn't playing or didn't understand decisions pertaining to myself, I would approach the coach about that and ask what I could do better. I certainly wouldn't ever question his decisions though.

How often did you train, and how did you manage school during this time as well?
Adriana: We trained five days per week and played on the weekends, all while trying to do our year twelve VCE (Victorian Certificate of Education) studies.

    Melissa: I remember being at training the night before an exam. We were asked at training why we were there when we had an English exam the next morning. We always organised ourselves to ensure we were prepared for our exams without having to skip training sessions. We used our free class times productively. We had no choice! While everyone else listened to music and chatted, we had our heads in our books studying. I remember, on one specific day, our PE teacher at the time acknowledged, in a concerning way, how hard we worked. We explained to her that due to our heavy football schedule, we had no choice. We weren't prepared to sacrifice our education because, at the end of the day, it's your lifeline. It was a very busy time, but it was worth it.

    Adriana: As hard as it was trying to keep up with everything at that time, football was also a form of release for us. When we're on the pitch, we aren't thinking about anything else, so ironically, while it can be stressful playing at a professional level, it's an activity which helps us manage our stress levels. Football helped us get through it.

    Melissa: The crazy thing is a lot of kids put all their time and effort into a sport and neglect their education because they think they are going to play professionally. Even if you do 'make it', sadly, sports like football are a short-lived career because eventually it catches up with your body. You need your education to fall back on later.

    Adriana: Stability is important, and that's where education comes in. It is so important! That's your lifeline. The other thing too is that if you are a young female playing in the A-League, you can't rely on your football income alone. You need to have another career to help you pay your mortgage and keep up with other living expenses too.

Do you think this is because you're both female?
Both: Yes.

    Adriana: I acknowledge there are other factors contributing to the reasons why we don't get the same pay as the men, but it is annoying to know that if I was a male playing at a professional level, football would be my full-time job. Instead, I need to have another job, which I love, but being able to play and dedicate my time to football full time would be my dream.

Did you experience any major setbacks during your professional career?
Melissa: Yes. Our second season with Melbourne Victory was a lot better. We were much more confident going into the season, felt more valued and the team chemistry had grown. It felt like it was our time to excel. The season was ours to win, then we had our first game in Adelaide, and I ruptured my ACL (anterior cruciate ligament) in the first four minutes of the game. I was so upset because, going into that season, I felt like it was the year I was going to get recognised as a key player in women's football. The year we were going to go on to do great things.

Adriana: I replaced Mel in that game, but I don't even remember much of it at all. I just kept thinking about my sister. When I found out the extent of Mel's injury after the game, I was distraught. I was more upset than she was. Poor Mel was the one with the injury, yet she was the one trying to comfort me. We have never not played together, and neither one of us had experienced a serious injury before, so I didn't know how to deal with it.

Melissa: This was also very tough on our family, who were back home in Melbourne watching the game on TV when I suffered the injury. We come from a big, close Italian family and extended relatives were at my parents' house watching the game. My parents were beside themselves when I came off the pitch, and they were trying to ring me, but of course, I couldn't answer because doctors were treating my knee. Eventually when I was able to contact them, my mum was crying. As a netball player, she had experienced an ACL injury too, so she understood what the next few months were going to be like for me. My leg was strapped, I was given crutches and we flew back from Adelaide to Melbourne.

What happened once you arrived home, and how were you feeling?
Melissa: I went to the doctors, got scans and began getting treatment.

A serious injury like that changes you. You think football is your life, and you give it everything. You just feel like your life is over, and you can't live anymore. I remember constantly asking, *"Why? Why now? Why? Why? Why?"*

How did you get through that?
Adriana: We had just finished school, and we were at university. I was enrolled in a Bachelor of Teaching and Mel was doing a Bachelor of Criminology.

Melissa: I did four weeks at university and realised it wasn't for me, so I left that. I had surgery and spent a lot of time in rehabilitation. I was not in a good place. I wasn't studying because I hadn't identified what I wanted to do. I couldn't work, and I couldn't play football. I was at home crying with my mum every day, wondering what I was going to do with my life. Looking back, it was probably the hardest year of my life, but I'm also a big believer that things happen for a reason.

I think the most important thing to remember during tough times is nothing bad lasts forever. Things always get better; you just need to give it time. I remember I would go to training and put on a fake smile. Everyone would come up to me and say, *"Don't worry, you're going to be fine. You'll come back even stronger."* I didn't believe it at the time, but the truth is, I did.

I also worked hard to recover. I did everything I could. One day I would focus on doing ten repetitions of tensing my leg. The next day I would go to the gym. My focus was on what I could do, not what I couldn't do. I had the will not just to come back but to come back stronger.

Adriana: The worst thing for me was I still had to get up, get my bag, head off to training and endure the trip on my own for the first time. Going to training and to my games that year was hard. Up until then, I had always played with my sister. I struggled not having her by my side. I tend to put more pressure on myself when my sister isn't playing with me. When she's playing, it's almost like I can share the pressure with her, but when she's not there, I feel like I carry it all myself. However, you must be strong, put one foot in front of the other and keep going. That's life.

We had each other's backs too. If I was going to the gym, I would ask her if she had done her exercises that day. I would check in on her regularly.

Melissa: Without my sister's support, it would've been a lot harder for me to get through that time.

Adriana: As time went on, we could witness the comeback. It was inspiring to watch. I still remember when she started training with the physiotherapists on the sideline next to where the rest of the team trained.

How long did it take before you were able to get back to playing?
Melissa: It took fifteen months before I was able to play a competitive game again. I missed two Women's A-League seasons and one National Premier League (NPL) season. It was a long road, but with persistence, I got there.

Adriana: On the other hand, I had a good season. We did a lot better than the previous year, and I continued to maintain a confident attitude. The team still had a lot to learn, but we were coming together nicely, and I enjoyed the team I was in.

Mel, how did it feel playing your first game after such a long and tough couple of years recovering?
Melissa: Physically, I felt awful. I was unfit. After an injury, it feels like you're never fully rehabilitated until after you start playing. Playing is the real test, and I had a lot of pain

PART 3: GOING PRO

in both knees during my entire first season back. I even had hamstring issues. It was a slow process.

The first game where I started was when we played with Calder United. All of my family was there, and they made a sign for me. It was great. The most amazing feeling ever! It reminded me why I play, for pure love of the game.

Looking back, I realise it took me an entire NPL season plus more to get my fitness back.

You both mention playing in the NPL; when was this, and who did you play with?
Adriana: At the end of each A-League season, we always played the off-season with an NPL team. While Mel was still recovering from her injury, I went to play my off-season with a new team in Geelong called 'Geelong Galaxy'. Two of our coaches from Melbourne Victory were the coaches for this new team, and they wanted us to be part of what they were building.

I remember initially thinking, *There's no way I'm travelling all the way to Geelong!* However, after more discussion with the coaches, who we already knew and loved from Melbourne Victory, we realised their plans and vision, and we decided to take the offer. We also discovered travelling all the way to Geelong wasn't taking any more time than our current trips to Melbourne Victory's training grounds. We had a good season with this team. We made it to the Grand Final. Unfortunately, we ended up losing though.

After your stint in Geelong, did you go back to Melbourne Victory again for the A-League season?
Adriana: I had to trial again, but Mel was still recovering from her injury, so she wasn't able to, therefore wasn't signed. I was offered a scholarship contract which meant, unlike my previous season with them, I could only train with the first team. That was hard for me because I thought I deserved a professional contract. However, a decision was made to take two wingers and only one midfielder. Unfortunately, I wasn't chosen, and I was told the day before my NPL final. My head was a mess.

Melissa: My head was a mess as well because I knew where she stood, how she must have been feeling, and I felt she deserved a spot on that team too.

Adriana: We had to go out and train that very same day I was given the news. We were both angry, but because of that, we trained well. In fact, I started to really enjoy my training sessions again because I was able to go out and give it my all without feeling any added pressure. I was determined to prove the selectors wrong, and it got to a point where highly regarded senior players on the team questioned why I didn't have a contract.

How did you deal with this setback?
Adriana: The positive was I started to get my life back a bit. I spent some weekends at the beach and watching games. Even though I wasn't playing, the girls still made me feel very much part of the team, so I didn't mind going and watching them.

I didn't let their decision kill my confidence either. Deep down, I knew I was good enough. The reality is everyone has different opinions on each of the players, and tough decisions have to be made in sport. I understand that, and this is why I don't hold anything against Melbourne Victory. I loved my time there, and they did so much in terms of helping me develop. I'm grateful for the experience we were given. In the end, I decided it was time for me to move on and seek out my next opportunity.

So where did you go from there?
Adriana: We remained at Melbourne Victory for the rest of the season, training and maintaining our fitness, then in the off-season, we were invited to train with Melbourne City. We decided to accept that invitation while we were both studying at university. Yes, Mel was back at university too!

The only problem was Melbourne City's training sessions were held in the morning, and I was on work placement as part of my university degree. Thankfully, I had a very understanding and supportive workplace, so I was able to start a bit later.

Eventually, Melbourne City pulled us all into a room and told us they wouldn't be offering anymore contracts, only scholarships. I remember Mel and I looking at each other, confused. I realised we were sacrificing work, income and university placements to train only. We were at a crossroads, and we needed to re-think our future, what we wanted and what was best for each of us. By this stage we were nineteen years old, and we felt we wanted some stability. We saw the year through training with Melbourne City and then with Geelong. After that we went to Calder United.

Did Calder United become your new club?
Melissa: Mark Torcaso was the coach at Calder United, and he had been trying to poach us for a long time. Often after we played against his team, he would approach us and ask us when we were going to go play for him. He was determined to have us on his team, and we used to joke with him and tell him to *"keep dreaming"*. Eventually, Mark won the battle and so we made our debut with Calder United.

Adriana: It was the best football decision we have ever made, by far! It was the best time I'd ever had playing football, the best club I'd ever played for and the best team I'd ever played with. We had a talented group; our friendships were strong, and football became fun again.

Melissa: There was a real community feel at the club. I could turn up right now, and it will still feel like home, like I'm with family.

PART 3: GOING PRO

Adriana: The amazing people we met through this club and the success we had was thrilling. The culture was second to none!

Melissa: If I had a bad day, I would look forward to going to training because I knew it would cheer me up in an instant.

We didn't struggle to get game time, and we felt valued again. It was like we were re-living the fun we experienced in our junior days. My confidence soared and the more confidence you have, the better you play.

Ironically, we played a league lower than the A-League, yet we enjoyed our football so much more. Sometimes you need to take a step back, rebuild your confidence, surround yourself with the right people and immerse yourself in the right culture to rise again. That is what Calder United did for us.

Did you go back to an A-League club after the NPL season with Calder Cannons?
Adriana: We had been in the system long enough to know that if we trained hard and proved ourselves, we could still be offered a contract with Melbourne City, and we've always had the mentality that if someone doesn't see our worth, we make it our business to prove them wrong. Despite our best efforts, we couldn't part with the feeling we still weren't going to progress at Melbourne City.

That realisation must have been tough. What did you do to cope with that?
Adriana: We were both starting to feel depleted, so it seemed timely that my parents rang and told us they were planning a trip to America and asked us if we wanted to join them. The trip was planned for November/December, over a three-week period. We knew this would mean we wouldn't be able to play in the A-League. Perhaps Melbourne City was planning on giving us a contract, but there was no certainty and Melbourne Victory hadn't invited us back for trials. We were in limbo. We decided to make the difficult decision to take the holiday, and it was the best decision we made. For a short time, we didn't think about football at all. I realise now how important it is to take a break from time to time to avoid burnout.

When we returned from America, we started training with Calder United again for the NPL season and, just like the rest of the world, we were struck with COVID-19 and subsequent lockdowns. In that year, we played one game, and the season was cancelled. That was tough. We went from seeing our teammates, who were like our family, four days a week to not at all. We would Zoom once per week, but it wasn't the same. I'm sure many kids around the world felt the same.

Melissa: That year was good for me because it gave me the opportunity to do a lot of gym work and continue to rebuild the strength and fitness I still lacked following my injury. The break worked well for me; so much so, that the season after the COVID-19 lockdown was the first season I played following my injury where I didn't feel any pain.

Yes, COVID-19 was a difficult time for many. What was it like for you when you were finally able to get back to playing?

Adriana: The year we returned to football following the lockdown, we had another successful season with Calder United. We were a talented team and won everything.

Melissa: The president at Calder United is an amazing woman who has done so much for women in football. She contacted us and told us about this new team being built called 'Western United', and that Calder United was in the process of building a partnership with them. In the words of Mark Torcaso, we were told that *"Exciting things were coming!"*

Adriana: We didn't play in the A-League that season. Instead, we spent some time at our family beach house and took a much-needed break after a successful NPL season. We were also still studying at university and working, so we were busy.

Western United created a development squad which involved professional-style training once per week. We were both selected for that together with quite a few of our Calder United teammates and some players from other clubs. It was also an opportunity for coaches at Western United to identify who they thought could potentially make up their first women's A-League squad.

As this was happening, I suffered my first big injury playing a game when I was kicked in the leg. I broke my fibula bone.

Melissa: It was at this time I realised just how bad Adriana must have felt for me when I had my injury, because now, it was exactly how I was feeling. I had to step up and provide her with the same level of support she gave me.

So, what is worse? Being the injured person or the person seeing their sister injured?

Both: Being the sister, for sure.

Adriana: I didn't need surgery. I was just put into a boot and ordered to rest for a few weeks, but it was a race against time because I knew the A-League season was approaching. I wanted to be healed and ready in time so that I would have a chance. Mentally, it was a really challenging time. Thankfully, Mark, our coach, and Amanda, the president at Calder United, took a chance on us and signed both of us with Western United.

What did you do to help yourself cope mentally during this time?

Adriana: I kept myself busy. I went to the gym and did the exercises I could do. I was working by this stage as a teacher as well, so I immersed myself in my work. I would go to training and to the games and watch the girls, which helped a lot. They were really supportive, and I found I could help by motivating them and giving them confidence. I wanted them to win. That's what got me through.

PART 3: GOING PRO

How long did it take for you to recover and return to football?
Adriana: Although the Western United physiotherapist told me we could realistically aim to have me back playing by the second game of the season, I was back by the first day of pre-season.

What sort of contract were you offered with Western United?
Melissa: The most exciting thing was that eleven of our teammates at Calder United got a contract with Western United. We were both promoted and given a professional contract all together. It felt like a dream!

Were there any players who didn't get a contract, and how did that make you feel?
Both: Yes.
Adriana: That's always tough, but the ones who didn't get a contract were still young and probably needed a couple more years in the NPL to get some more experience and develop. I think everyone who got a contract was expecting one. I don't think there were any surprises.

How did it feel to finally get that professional contract at a time when you felt ready?
Melissa: It felt so good, but it's not long before you start thinking about the next challenge. How do I get selected to play or, better still, be in the starting eleven?
Adriana: Luckily for us, for our first game, we walked out in the starting eleven together. We played against Melbourne Victory, managed by the coach who didn't select us, and we won 1–0. I must admit, it was a good feeling.
Melissa: After the game, the Melbourne Victory coach approached us and told us he was really happy to see us there. We expressed our gratitude towards him for everything he had taught us. In hindsight, I think he made the right decision not to select us back then. We weren't ready then like we were with Western United. It's very important not to burn bridges and to maintain healthy relationships in any career.

What was your first season like at Western United?
Melissa: We ended up on a nine-week winning streak and came runner-up in the Grand Final. Eleven of us on that team came from Calder United, and many of us had never played in the A-League before, yet we achieved such great results. I attribute our success to the level of chemistry we already had from playing together in previous years. It was one of the best experiences we've ever had!

However, although we were experiencing such highs, there were days of immense pressure, frustration and anger too. We constantly fought to be selected to play. That felt overwhelming, but we understand that's how sport works.

I remember one day seeing Adriana at work and saying to her, *"We need to remember to have fun."* We remind each other of this from time to time. If you don't remind yourself of this, you can begin to hate it.

Adriana: I was working as a teacher in a school that values sports during my first season in the A-League with Western United. Thankfully, the school was very supportive and did everything to accommodate me. I would train with Western United in the morning, then rush off to school and get there during recess right before the next period. It was hectic.

Melissa: Sometimes, I would be at work and start to feel a bit of pain in my leg. Automatically I would start to analyse everything. *Have I had enough water today? Am I eating the right things? Why am I sore? I need to play tomorrow.* All these things can weigh heavily on you. The mental stress from overthinking everything gets exhausting.

Adriana: When you reach the end of the season, you think to yourself, *Thank God, I got through it,* and you breathe a sigh of relief. Perhaps that's just because we put too much pressure on ourselves, but I'm sure many other players do too, and that's why it's so important to remind yourself to just enjoy it. If you're enjoying it, you are more likely to play well. I can't stress this enough.

Now, I tell people I feel like I'm living my dream. I'm working as a teacher, and I'm playing the sport I love at the level I want to play at.

Melissa: The road to get to that point is long, and you must endure so many ups and downs, but I believe everything happens for a reason. Everything that happened to us, including the injury to my ACL, led us to where we are today. At the end of it all, the ups and downs we experienced have contributed to the development of our resilience.

Is there any dream of going overseas?
Melissa: Yes. I have visited Italy because that's where my family is from. It's certainly something I would be open to. On top of that, our favourite style of play is that of European football, so I feel it would suit us. I haven't tried to look for it, but if it was presented to me, I would consider it.

Adriana: At this stage I'm loving life here though, and we come from a very close-knit family, so I'm not sure. It's not always about status or money. We're only here for a short time, so it's important to be happy and enjoy your life too. There's more to life than football!

What does your typical day look like now and where to next for the Taranto girls?
Adriana: Our day is hectic. We get up at 6:00 a.m., drive to Werribee, train, go to the gym, go to work (as schoolteachers), come home, make dinner, then walk the dog.

In terms of where to next**,** my goal now is to make a name for myself in the A-League.

Melissa: Me too. We want to be key players in the league.

PART 3: GOING PRO

Do you feel you both 'made it'?

Both: Yes, especially following the successful season we just had!

Melissa: I often can't believe it when I get asked for an autograph. I think, *Really? Me?*

Adriana: People know us, and we are proud of that, especially given the challenging road it takes to reach such a point.

What advice would you give to young kids today?

Both: Enjoy the game!

Adriana: If you're on the bench, don't worry. Just keep trying, keep pushing at training sessions to prove your coach wrong. Do not turn up with your head down and moping. Make your coach think, *Maybe I got that wrong.* Stay ready so that you don't have to get ready.

Melissa: Sometimes, what makes you feel so great is simply being part of a team, not necessarily the skills you can demonstrate on a pitch.

Joshua Risdon

"Whether it's winning a local championship or the World Cup, what makes it special is who you are experiencing it with. The journey you go on with your teammates and the memories you make, for me, far outweighs any individual achievement."

What happened after your first season with the Perth Glory Youth Team?
Josh: During pre-season, which ran from May to October, a few of my teammates and I were asked to join the first team for training.

What's it like being asked to train with the first team at a professional level?
Josh: It's a pinch-me moment and nerve-racking, of course. I remember Robbie Fowler (former Liverpool FC star) was on the team at the time, and I couldn't believe I was training with him. I was a bit star-struck. In saying that, I've always been blessed with a very hard-working, grounded mentality that my parents passed on to me, and because I was already playing with men, I was used to the physicality and presence of older players.

What was your mindset like going into that first training session?
Josh: You don't want to make any mistakes, that's for sure. I was very quiet and thought to myself, *If I do well, this could be my chance.* Thankfully, I performed really well, and halfway through pre-season training, I was offered my first contract with the first team.

How did that feel?
Josh: I will always remember the moment the coach pulled me aside and told me he was offering me a professional contract with the first team. It was one of the greatest moments. Unreal. I was buzzing.

It came at a good time too because I had left my cooking job at Sizzlers, so I was currently unemployed. I was applying for jobs but hadn't got anything yet. Getting the offer at this time allowed me to breathe a sigh of relief. It was my lifeline.

Who was the first person you told?
Josh: My parents, of course. They were so happy for me.

PART 3: GOING PRO

Was the income from your first contract enough to cover your living expenses at the time?
Josh: Before getting my first pro contract, I still relied on my parents a bit. That's why I was looking for jobs, but once I got the professional contract, that was when I was able to start supporting myself independently. I wasn't living a lavish lifestyle, the kind that is often portrayed in the media. In fact, I remember turning up to games in a 'banged-up' Hyundai Elantra. The older, more established players would turn up in their Mercedes and other high-end vehicles. My dad used to tease me about it. Eventually, I bought myself a decent car; however, up until today, my dad reminds me of that time. He says, *"At least you're driving a decent car to the stadium now!"*

People think that because you're a professional player, you're earning big dollars, but it takes time to get to that stage, if you ever do.

What was your debut like with the Perth Glory first team?
Josh: I wasn't in the starting eleven, and I didn't get my debut until later in the season, when our numbers were a bit short due to injuries and a red card. It was the fifth-last game of the season, and the coach approached me during the week and told me I was going to start that weekend. We were playing in North Queensland, and I was extremely nervous, but I still managed to perform well. I'm lucky I can perform well under pressure. I must admit, once the games start, the nerves ease off a bit.

What I didn't see coming was that, despite what I may have looked like on the outside, playing at this level triggered a feeling of anxiety that got quite bad, particularly in the lead-up to each game. I began to suffer internally.

Why do you think you were feeling so anxious, and how did you manage that?
Josh: The pressure was intense, and I put so much pressure on myself too. I didn't speak to anyone about it and kept it bottled up, which wasn't the right thing to do.

Is that because you thought that if you did speak out, it could jeopardise your career?
Josh: Yeah, and I was only eighteen or nineteen years old. Back then, there was a bit more of a stigma attached to mental health as well. The good thing now is everyone is so open about it and that stigma has gone. It's very common, and it's seen as normal.

So how did you handle the pressures you felt and, consequently, the anxiety you experienced before you sought the right help?
Josh: Not very well. Although I never became an alcoholic, I started developing the bad habit of drinking more alcohol than I should have. It wasn't the right way to deal with it, and it certainly was not a permanent solution.

Looking back, I think anxiety has been something I have struggled with my entire career; however, I have now taken steps to deal with it properly.

Explain to me what the build-up of your anxiety looked like?
Josh: The way it worked was the anxiety would start building the day before a game, then it would increase on game day. By the end of the game, I was able to forget about it. Thankfully, I was still able to perform while I was on the pitch, but I still clearly remember one game where I faked an injury two minutes into the second half because I couldn't take it anymore. It got too debilitating.

How did you manage to get through your first season while you were dealing with this?
Josh: I just pushed through. I had to. I was relieved when the season finished though because I knew I didn't have to worry about another game for a while.

What happened in the lead-up to the commencement of your second season?
Josh: I didn't start in the first eleven at the beginning of the second season. I was nineteen years old at this time. However, after round four, the player who was playing in the right back position suffered an injury, so I ended up playing every game from round five.

Was the anxiety under control during your second season?
Josh: No. It was still the same, and I wasn't managing it well. I developed this mindset that I didn't care anymore.

Did football start to feel more like a job and less fun?
Josh: Definitely. I was very naïve going into this career. I was oblivious to the real level of pressure. I didn't know anything about it, and I didn't know anyone who had taken this path before me. There were moments when I felt like I just wanted to give it all away and go back home to Bunbury, especially when I was feeling high levels of anxiety.

Were you able to open up by speaking to your family?
Josh: I could've spoken to my family, and I did at times, but only when it got to a point when the anxiety had built up so much and got so intense I felt like I had to say something to someone. My parents didn't know how bad it really was.

How did you perform in that second season with Perth Glory, especially with all the struggles you experienced internally?
Josh: I don't know how, but I managed to continue to play well. We made the Grand

PART 3: GOING PRO

Final. We lost, but it was a close game. I was awarded our team 'Player of the Year', and I also got 'Players Player of the Year'. I was nineteen years old, and the rest of the team were twenty-four years old and over. I achieved all of this while I struggled so much internally. Succeeding at this time probably wasn't the best thing for me though, because I thought I could just keep suffering quietly and managing my anxiety ineffectively.

I'm sure you have regrets looking back, so what are some of them?
Josh: Apart from not taking the right steps to manage my anxiety better, I regret (that) I was not only numbing the immense pressure but also some of the greatest moments too. I robbed myself of many times when I should have felt a sense of genuine happiness and utter joy.

I developed this persona amongst my teammates that I was the life of the party, but not in a good way. They probably thought I just liked going out and being silly, but unbeknownst to them, I dealt with something far more serious. I was trying to cope, and I was doing it by trying to escape from my true feelings every weekend.

At some point, did this lifestyle start to have a negative impact on your career?
Josh: My performance started to decline in my third year in the first team at Perth Glory. I didn't have a great season, and I distinctly remember having a bad game halfway through that season. My dad asked me if I thought I was partying too much. The answer was *"Yes."* He told me to cut it back a bit, and I did. As a result, I ended up having a better end to the season, but I still hadn't addressed my anxiety.

How did you eventually address your anxiety?
Josh: I didn't address it properly until 2021. It's important to know that if you don't deal with things properly, eventually they will catch up on you.

So, from your third year at Perth Glory until 2021, how did you push on and progress?
Josh: Meeting my wife helped immensely. I met her in Perth when I was twenty and she was eighteen. It was during my third season at Perth Glory.

I also started to find better ways of managing my anxiety and got better at it. There were times when it would build up, but they were getting further and further apart. Until I found out the deeper reason, this continued from the age of twenty-two to twenty-eight.

What was the deeper reason and how did you eventually rekindle the joy that you once had when you started playing as a child?
Josh: There are a lot of things contributing to finding that level of joy again. I think the

biggest thing for me was seeing a sport psychologist for a year or two, and through that, I worked out I had an athletic identity. I put so much pressure on myself to perform because my whole self-value was based on how I would perform as a football player. I had always been known as 'Josh, the football player', and I never really figured out who I was outside of football.

I used to think that if I made a mistake on the pitch, no one was going to like me anymore. It seems silly, but that's how I felt. Now, I feel like I have separated my athletic identity from who I am. It's my job and I can go home at the end of the day and be a good dad to my kids. A bad game isn't going to make me a different person.

I think everything happens for a reason though. It's been a long journey, but I believe I had to go through everything I did to get to where I am now.

What's it like for a partner of an elite athlete?
Josh: My wife is a great support and understood early on that football had to come first. This is the case for any elite athlete in any sport. You can't underestimate the sacrifices partners make for elite athletes. They give up their jobs and time with their families to travel around the world with you, following your career. Sometimes you feel a sense of guilt, and that's another pressure you can carry.

When I moved to Sydney and started playing for Western Sydney Wanderers, she came too. Her attitude was amazing. She looked at it like it was an adventure for us, and not so much about her following me because of my career. She wanted to move as much as I did and secured herself a job beforehand.

I can imagine that if you had a partner who didn't want to leave, it would be very hard.

As an athlete, I assume you have to eat a certain way, and if you're not cooking, is this something your partner has to think about?
Josh: I'm lucky in that my wife is a very healthy eater herself. She understood very quickly what it's like for me as an athlete and what my diet had to look like, but it wasn't a huge transition because of her own healthy lifestyle. She's incredible in that way and has been very supportive from the moment I met her.

What are some of the downsides to playing at a professional level that kids may not know or understand?
Josh: There's no stability. You don't know if your contract is going to be renewed from year to year, and that's your livelihood—your income to be able to live. It's a constant fight to keep your spot.

To be specific, there's a period when there are approximately ten games left in the season, and players haven't been told yet if they're getting another contract. Ten weeks seems like a long time, but it's not. It goes very quickly. Some players get to the very end of the season, and they are told *"No, we are not offering you another contract."* Suddenly, they are left wondering what they are going to do next.

I've seen so many players get caught in that position without a backup plan, and to be clear, having a backup plan is not always easy when you have to be so focused on your football career. It's for this reason you must have an innate genuine love and passion for playing.

So how did you eventually become a Socceroo?
Josh: By the time I was twenty-three, I had settled down, chosen to focus more on my football development, and eased off on the bad habits. I had to deal with the anxiety. It was at this time I also saw a future with my girlfriend, who is now my wife.

I set my sights on becoming a Socceroo. They had two qualifying games coming up: one in Canberra and one in Bangladesh. The moment I was told I had been selected is a moment I will never forget. It was an amazing feeling. My parents were coming to visit me in Perth that weekend, so I decided to wait and tell them in person when they arrived. When I told them over dinner, my mum started crying and my dad got up and gave me a big hug. It was amazing! Not just for myself but for my mum and dad as well because they sacrificed so much for me over the years. I felt happy for them too.

That reminds me, back then I carried the pressures of the people around me, so when something paid off, I felt relieved and happy for everyone else, rather than for myself.

I think the first time I felt like everything had worked out and that the sacrifices I made for so many years finally paid off was when I played in my first World Cup in 2018. This was the moment I thought, *I made it.* It doesn't get any better or any bigger than that!

Is it true you left the country the day after you got married to attend the Socceroos' training camp?
Josh: Yes. Funnily enough we scheduled to have our wedding straight after the A-League Grand Final. We thought that was a safe bet because there weren't going to be any scheduled matches taking place afterwards, but we didn't anticipate I was going to get a call to attend the Socceroos' training camp. Football is like that though. You can't book anything in advance.

How did your debut into the Socceroos come about?
Josh: It was one week before my wedding when I got the call to be part of the squad of thirty players selected for the Socceroos' World Cup training camp. The camp was due

to start on our wedding day. I had to ask if I could arrive a couple of days late because I was getting married. Right up until the last minute, I didn't know if I was going to the camp or if I was going on a honeymoon. I had to pack for both scenarios.

They approved my request, so I got married on Saturday night and left my new wife on Sunday night for three weeks to attend the training camp. I didn't even know if I was going to form part of the final World Cup squad at this point because, from the thirty players attending the training camp, they could only choose twenty-three.

Did your wife join you overseas at some point?
Josh: Once I knew I had made the squad, she booked a flight and joined me, then we had our honeymoon afterwards.

What was your first World Cup game like?
Josh: I walked into the changerooms, saw my yellow jersey hanging with my name on the back, and thought, *Wow*. There are no words to describe that feeling. I guess you just feel so proud of yourself and everyone who helped you get to that point.

I remember my jersey hanging next to another player who I grew up with. He was in one of my State teams growing up and from Perth as well. He turned to me and said, *"Who would've thought a boy from Armidale and Bunbury, Western Australia, would be playing in the World Cup next to each other?"* We took a moment together to take it all in.

The whole lead-up to that game, including the lineup in the tunnel and hearing our country's national anthem, made me feel so excited, happy and confident. It's a surreal moment.

You say you felt confident. In what way?
Josh: I just felt like I was ready. It's what I had worked all my life for, and nothing was going to stop me or let me down now.

Were you in the starting eleven?
Josh: Yes, I was.

Did you play in the right back position?
Josh: Yes, I did.

Who was your opponent?
Josh: We played against France. In the first half, I played against Ousmane Dembele, and in the second half, I played against Kylian Mbappe.

PART 3: GOING PRO

They are very tough opponents. Australia was proud of the team's performance, but how do you feel your team played?

Josh: I think we played well, and we should have got a result, but France won and, ultimately, went on to win that World Cup. Despite the loss, that game is probably the greatest highlight of my career.

I think there's this perception (that) it's tough playing against some of the world's best players and teams, and it is, but when you're out there on the pitch, you see the gap is not that big. We were competitive.

Did you feel star-struck at all playing against the likes of Mbappe and Giroud?

Josh: I was a bit. It was very surreal. There was a moment when I thought to myself, *What's this small-town boy from Bunbury doing here playing football in a World Cup?*

What was your next move after you returned from the 2018 World Cup?

Josh: I moved to Melbourne. I was one of the first players to sign for Western United when the team was formed, and I became a regular starting eleven player, which felt great.

You won a championship with Western United. What was that like?

Josh: We won the 2021–22 championship. To be honest, that feeling was probably even better than playing in the World Cup because I could see how much joy it brought to so many other people. Being able to bring joy to others is important to me and something that makes me genuinely happy. I feel like it's my meaning in life now. To be able to help contribute to winning the trophy and to witness the heartfelt emotions of others by winning felt unbelievable. I feel I have a special and strong, lifelong bond with the team and the management of this team.

That was a very special year for me. Not only did we win the championship but I also learned how to manage my anxiety a lot better too.

Do you feel only elite players experience those kinds of emotions?

Josh: Absolutely not. Whether it's winning a local championship or the World Cup, what makes it special is who you are experiencing it with. The journey you go on with your teammates and the memories you make, for me, far outweighs any individual achievement.

What's it like being the captain, and how do you cope with that added pressure?

Josh: There is more pressure being in a leadership role. I feel like I put a lot of pressure on myself to make sure the team is in a good headspace. You want to make sure everything is going well. In 2022, we didn't do too well, and I would often blame myself. I questioned what I was doing wrong.

Do you have other players come to you for advice or support if they're struggling?
Josh: Yes, particularly the younger players, who understandably seek support from time to time.

What do you say to aspiring athletes who ask you what they can do to get noticed or to get more game time?
Josh: I tell them to keep working hard and reassure them their chance will come if they keep at it. They need to keep pushing and working hard because they need to be ready for when that chance comes along.

Have you seen anyone become distraught from being dropped?
Josh: Yeah, I have. There are always players who aren't happy when they're not playing. It can get to them, and then they start to second-guess themselves. The self-doubt kicks in. It's so hard because each week there're always players who aren't going to play.

How do you feel about your career now?
Josh: For me, I loved playing football as a kid, and I saw a way of having a future in it. At one point, it did become a job I disliked a bit, but now I'm back at the point of loving it again, just as I did when I was a child. I really appreciate everything I have done and enjoy knowing I can play football for a living.

It's not an easy career. I'm thirty-one now and still going through different strategies to see what works best for me in preparing for an upcoming game. I'm constantly just trying to figure it out, and that's part of the journey. I wouldn't change it for the world, but it's been hard.

PART 3: GOING PRO

Chloe Logarzo

*"In the 2019 World Cup,
I finally just played for me."*

You got your first professional contract in Sweden. What made you go to Sweden?
Chloe: The league is good, so it's a very good pathway for Australians. They love Australians over there too.

What was the expectation of that club?
Chloe: I came in at the back end of the season, so the team had already been formed. The plan was for me to stay for four months to help them progress in the Champions League. The expectation was I was going to slide into the team and score lots of goals for them. This didn't happen. I was exhausted, having just come back from the Olympics, but did quite well regardless. I played a lot while I was there.

What was your position?
Chloe: At that time, I played left wing.

Did they speak English?
Chloe: It was the first time I played in a foreign country where the language was different; however, the players spoke English to me. It was the coach who didn't like to speak English, so that was challenging.

The first game we played was away. I remember getting my hair cut when I got a call from one of my teammates who said, *"Chloe, where are you?"* I replied with, *"What do you mean?"* She went on to say, *"We're on the bus waiting for you!"* I thought we had a home game. The team spoke to each other in Swedish, which I didn't understand, and no one had told me we were playing away, so I thought I could get my hair cut the day before the game. I quickly realised we were driving to an away game the day before and not playing at home.

In Sweden, they take us by bus to all away games. Bus rides could be anywhere from three to eight hours.

What did you do?
Chloe: Luckily, I lived close enough to be able to walk to my training facility. I was probably 600 metres away. I grabbed my bike, and off I went with only half of my hair cut. I had never ridden my bike so fast in all my life. I got on the bus, and everyone was

looking at me. I was so embarrassed, and I just said, *"Sorry, I lost my keys!"* I didn't know what else to say. That was a bad experience, and I didn't want to leave a negative first impression, particularly on the coaches.

Did you have any other challenges?
Chloe: On top of that, I had to learn the Swedish currency, and for the very first time, I had to train in the snow with a beanie on. That was interesting.

What happened at the end of your season with Eskilstuna United?
Chloe: I played the remainder of the season, but in the second-to-last game that year, a girl stepped on my ankle, and I got a syndesmosis injury. I needed surgery, so I flew back to Australia. When I arrived in Sydney, I got a connecting flight to Adelaide. I went there because they can get you in and out of surgery quicker when you're with the national team, so the recovery is quicker.

It was a long, tough flight back home, but it was the best thing for me. In Sweden, they didn't want to send me for a scan, so they didn't know what was wrong with me. I'm not sure if they cared or not because I couldn't play for them in the Champions League anymore, which is what they were really focused on at the time.

That's how my time in Sweden came to an end.

How long did it take for you to recover from the injury?
Chloe: I was out for five months.

Did you struggle to return to football after that?
Chloe: As I was coming back to the Matildas, we had a tournament in Portugal. I told them I had a little bit of pain in my ankle. It turned out I had a stress fracture because I came back too soon from the syndesmosis injury. This prevented me from playing even longer, and instead of playing in Portugal, I was in a little basement undergoing rehabilitation.

When did you return to football?
Chloe: After Portugal, I came back to Australia, and after not having played at all in the second season with Newcastle United, I decided I wanted to return to Sydney FC again. Thankfully I was welcomed back and played a season with them.

Where did you go after that season?
Chloe: After that season, I decided to play for a team in Norway. I was with Emily Gielnik. Ellie Carpenter came and lived with us for three months as well when she was sixteen years old. She just trained because she was too young to sign a professional

contract. Then all three of us went to a club together called Avaldsnes.

We played there for ten months in the Champions League.

What is it like playing in the Champions League?
Chloe: It was great, but the team struggled a bit. When we got to the round of sixteen and had to face Barcelona, we ended up losing 4–0.

Given you were overseas, did you struggle with language barriers again?
Chloe: Everyone can speak English in Norway like in Sweden. They just choose not to. When I lived in Norway, I lived in a household with seven people. Four Brazilians and three Australians. Everyone in the house was in the starting lineup. There were a couple of games that went wrong, and the coach decided we were losing because he was speaking English. From then on, he started speaking Norwegian. All seven of us, plus an American, who made up the first eleven, had no idea what he was saying.

What were the living conditions like?
Chloe: It was very small for the number of people living there.
Everyone in this household trains together, goes home together, then gets up together. Sometimes I craved space but couldn't get it.

What other challenges did you face in Norway?
Chloe: One day we were playing Barcelona, and I had a disagreement with the coach. He brought me all the way to Barcelona and made me sit in the grandstand, not even on the bench. He didn't roster me to play at all, and he didn't let me know in advance.

I was putting my full kit on when the goalkeeper coach came over to me and said, *"Did he not tell you?"* I asked, *"Tell me what?"* He replied, *"That you're not playing."* I couldn't believe it. I had played every game, so I couldn't understand. I was so upset I made the decision to leave the club.

Were you able to break your contract?
Chloe: I told the owner of the club what happened, and we came to a mutual agreement. That's how I was able to get out of that contract.

Were you getting paid a decent amount of money at this stage?
Chloe: Not at all.
As a player, you want to be in the starting eleven in countries with professional leagues to increase your chances at playing at the highest level, but the women's pay is not great at all.

Did you come back to Australia?
Chloe: Yes, I did, and I went back to Sydney FC.

One thing I will never forget is playing for Sydney FC in the 2018–19 season Grand Final. There were five minutes to go, and we were winning 4–3 or 4–2. A girl gets subbed on for Perth Glory (Sam Kerr's team). Her first touch was heavy, so I went to toe poke the ball away from her, and she kicked my leg instead of the ball. I fractured my fibula. I was on the ground screaming. I was shattered because 2019 was the year of the next FIFA Women's World Cup.

What did you do?
Chloe: I had scans done but nothing was showing up. I even had bone stress tests. My results were consistent with a fracture or break. I also had nerve damage.

Because of football, I've torn my ACL, had a plate put in my collarbone, now have a tightrope in my ankle and a pin in my toe, but nothing compares to the pain of nerve damage. I couldn't turn over in bed without being in extreme agony. It took approximately two weeks before I could get up and walk around.

At that time, I was put on an AlterG, which is like an anti-gravity treadmill. It takes away a portion of your body weight. I was running at 20 per cent of my body weight, which is nothing, like I'm on the moon. I kept getting doctors' opinions, and I started to think maybe it was all in my head because they all kept telling me it was just nerve damage. I was using an expensive machine for chronic nerve injury patients, but nothing worked. Eventually, I went to another doctor. When she examined my knee, she held it right above where I got kicked and proceeded to do a bone stress test. I heard *'Bang',* which was the sound of my leg breaking! Turned out I had a spiral fracture which doesn't show up in scans.

At least now you knew what the issue was. What happened from there?
Chloe: I was put into a Moon Boot for the first time, then once I came out of the boot, I started intense rehabilitation. I worked so hard. I had a stationary bike in the front room of my parents' house. In front of the bike, on the wall, I had a picture of the World Cup trophy. I cycled every single morning staring at the World Cup trophy. I couldn't run, so that was my motivation.

When were you able to return to football?
Chloe: I didn't play a single game until I was at the Matildas' camp participating in a training game. I was only semi-healed, but I was determined to be the fittest person there. I just thought to myself that if I can't play, then at least I'll be able to offer that.

PART 3: GOING PRO

Did you play?
Chloe: In 2019, I went to my first FIFA World Cup in France.

I played the best I have played since Tokyo, and I scored my first World Cup goal against Brazil. In that game, I had an assist and a goal. We were down 2–0 and ended up winning 3–2. I was 'Player of the Match'. This was, by far, the highlight of my career.

I felt I had finally overcome so many hurdles, struggles and disappointments. Up until that moment I had always played with intentions of trying to prove people wrong. I wanted to play well because people weren't selecting me. I wanted to play well because the coach thought I wasn't good enough. I wanted to play well because I wasn't strong enough or big enough or because I let myself down. In the 2019 World Cup, I finally just played for me.

That's amazing! Did you go back to Sydney FC after the World Cup?
Chloe: No, I didn't. I went to America, which is where I was just before I was called up for the World Cup camp. I played for Washington Spirit. That's where I met my fiancée.

Why America?
Chloe: They have one of the best leagues. I would say they sit in the top three leagues in the world in women's football.

How was your experience in America?
Chloe: The American league is tough, so I only played five or six games. I spent a lot of time away from the team too because I was being called up to train and play with the Matildas. One time, I had to travel from America to Turkey for the Matildas' camp.

What's it like having to fly all the time?
Chloe: It's exhausting but I managed it. Back then I was flying economy. That was harder because I would need a few days to settle and adapt. These days, the team flies in business class, which means we can get off the plane and train on the same day.

Where did you go after America?
Chloe: After America, I came back home and played for Sydney FC but asked for a release so that I could go and play in England. They allowed that, so I went to England and played for Bristol City. That's when COVID-19 hit.

What about your fiancée? Did she come with you?
Chloe: When I heard England was going to be locked down, she came to where I was. She had retired from football by this stage.

What was your time like at Bristol City?

Chloe: I played almost a year with Bristol City; however, in the first transfer window, I got traded to Kansas City, so I went back to America. Kansas City bought out my contract, and I signed a three-year deal with them.

Moving to Kansas City wasn't easy because it was during COVID-19 times. It took me two months to leave England because I had to wait for my American visa to come through and the English embassy, who can help with that, was so busy during that time they couldn't help me. On top of that, I was kicked out of where I was living in Bristol because I wasn't a player anymore.

How did you stay fit in those two months?

Chloe: For the first month, Kansas City arranged for me to drive to St. Georges Park, which is where the English national team plays. I would stay there four days a week to train, then stay somewhere else for the other three days. Kansas City covered the cost because they wanted me to stay fit, but it was so expensive they were only able to do it for one month.

In the second month I was stuck in England, I stayed with a friend in London. I slept on her two-seater couch until I bought myself an inflatable single bed. I was staying fit by just running on the streets of London.

What happened when you finally arrived in Kansas City?

Chloe: As soon as I arrived, I was immediately thrust into training and games with the team. I played approximately five games with them, but then I had something wrong with my hip, toe and foot. I was a bit broken. I'm sure these 'niggles' came about because I wasn't training on proper surfaces while I was stuck in England and because I wasn't given a chance to ease back into training. As a result, I was in and out of the team at Kansas City.

Also, while I was at Kansas City, I went away with the Australian national team to Ireland for a couple of friendly matches. Sixty minutes into my second game, I tore my ACL. I went back to the United States and had surgery in Tampa, USA.

How long were you out for?

Chloe: I spent the next three months in Arizona doing the first portion of my rehab, then I went back to Australia to do the remaining three months. I spent six months away from the Kansas City team, then I returned to complete the remainder of my rehab. I was medically released after nine months.

Did you play with Kansas City again?

Chloe: I got back to full training and was doing well, but the coach never put me on the field, so I didn't get an opportunity to play with them again. The team made the final in that second season, but I didn't play a single game.

Did you leave?
Chloe: At this point, I had one more year left in my contract with Kansas City, so I arranged for them to provide me with a twelve-match loan to A-League club Western United in Australia. I figured that would take me through until my pre-season return with Kansas City for the third year of my contract.

I arrived at Western United and found the grounds we train on quite hard. I developed a condition in my feet called plantar fasciitis. It became so bad I couldn't walk in the mornings. It would take me forty minutes to be able to walk again after training. In the end, I had to see a specialist and have microsurgery done.

You've had to bounce back after many injuries. How did this latest injury impact your career?
Chloe: The next FIFA Women's World Cup was approaching, at home in Australia, a once-in-a-lifetime opportunity. I was freaking out at the thought of not making it into the Matildas' squad. This, for me, was a very special World Cup.

What happened?
Chloe: My foot finally got better, but I still wasn't playing any games. When the World Cup pre-camp commenced, I was called to attend. I went and got through every training session. I could feel I was starting to become fit again, and I was feeling good; however, I wasn't invited to attend the second round because I wasn't fit enough yet.

How did that feel?
Chloe: I was devastated. Heartbroken. I had been dreaming about this World Cup for three years. The fact it was at home made it so much more special too. Knowing I wasn't going to be part of something I had worked so hard for hurt immensely. I know a World Cup on home soil will never happen again, and I wasn't part of it. I have to live with that.

On top of that, seeing the Matildas make history at that World Cup and witnessing how life-changing it has been for each of the players has made it even harder for me to accept. I know it could've been me if I had been given a fraction more time.

That's the most frustrating thing. If I had been able to attend the second block of the pre-World Cup camp, which was only a couple of weeks away, I know I would've had my full fitness back. In the end, the coach was only able to go by my performance in that small window given.

I would've attended that World Cup wholeheartedly and given it everything I had, just like I did in 2019, but it wasn't to be.

How did you cope during the World Cup?
Chloe: I'm so grateful and blessed I was still able to be part of the World Cup in a broadcasting role with Optus Sport. I was on the panel talking at each of the Matildas' games, and I was on the ground broadcasting from the sidelines during them.

I didn't take my decision to commit to a broadcasting role lightly. I wanted to help connect the fans with the players as best I could; however, that was the hardest thing I've ever had to do. Watching the games and talking about them while feeling like I was missing out on playing felt crippling. I cried at every game and each time the Australian national anthem played.

Do you think you still have another World Cup left in you?
Chloe: I would like to think so, but who knows?

The disappointment of not being selected for the latest World Cup is still fresh.

Personally, I feel my output has been a lot greater than what I have gained in return in the last couple of years, and that can drive down motivation. I struggled for two years, then missed my home World Cup. It's going to take time to come back from that.

I have always been the type of player who needs a coach who believes in me. If I have that, then I believe I can get back into my best form.

Looking back over your career so far, do you feel like you 'made it'?
Chloe: Absolutely. Even when I didn't get chosen to play for the national team, I still feel like I made it.

Life as a professional footballer is like a triangle. There are three points, and each point represents something different. One point represents football, the other represents home and family, and the third represents where you are currently living. As a professional footballer, it is unlikely you will ever have all three points going well at the same time. For example, your family and home life may be doing well, and you may be doing well in football, but you may hate where you're living. Alternatively, you may love where you're living, and everything back home may be going well, but you might be playing terribly.

What would you tell a young kid today wanting to pursue football as a career?
Chloe: For me, I've always wanted to go and experience life in different countries, and I'm grateful I had the opportunity to do that through football. No matter what my bank account looked like at different times, I felt rich in life. I created friendships with people from all over the world I still have today.

I would stress to kids trying to make it that it's not going to be what you think and to know that when things aren't going in the direction you expect, allow yourself to take something else out of the situation you're in. Embrace the culture of the country you might be living in or be proud you might be living overseas by yourself and making new friends. If you do this, you will look back on your football career and be grateful for what it gave you. It doesn't matter if you play in the second division for a club overseas; you have achieved more than you would had you not stepped outside of your comfort zone.

Emily Gielnik

"I sacrificed so much, worked incredibly hard and did everything I could to get selected, and it still wasn't enough. With that said, that's life. Football success is often based on someone's opinion at the time."

What happened after you got selected for the Queensland Academy of Sport?
Emily: I got my first full-time contract in the women's A-League while I was in my first year at QAS. I was sixteen or seventeen years old. A week before the start of my first season with Brisbane Roar, I suffered from a stress fracture in my foot. That was my first major injury, and I missed my entire first season.

Take us through your return following your injury.
Emily: In my second year, I came back, and I was playing well, but it still wasn't easy.

My coach had me in the grandstand for the first few years at Brisbane Roar. I didn't even make the squad. All those feelings of self-doubt I had experienced as a junior came flooding back to me. I honestly felt that, at the very least, I should be on the bench, but I had to remain patient, particularly when there were so many Matildas on my team. I was up against some of the best players in the country. It was a hard time for me; however, I used this time to tap into my resilience and was motivated to prove myself to the coach. Many others chose to transfer to another team or not to play at all, but that wasn't me.

It got to a point where some of the players took it upon themselves to speak to the coach about giving me a chance. They felt I was deserving of it.

Eventually, I came off the bench for five or ten minutes. I made the most of those minutes and scored every single time I went on. Sometimes one goal, sometimes two. I started getting nicknamed the 'Super Sub', which was quite funny. In one season, which consisted of eight to twelve games, I scored twelve or thirteen goals, and I didn't even play ninety minutes of football in that whole year! However, that was a breakthrough year for me, and I became a starting eleven player from then on.

You really had to fight for game time. Why do you think that was?
Emily: Despite the struggle, I had a lot of respect for that coach because, even though I sometimes felt ready, there's always a lesson to be learned. For me it was maturing, earning my spot and instilling more fire in me. It also led to developing a lot of respect from my teammates too.

PART 3: GOING PRO

Did you see others struggle?
Emily: It wasn't easy. For those of us on this team, it felt like we were in a Matildas' camp every week because we had so many Matildas on this Brisbane team. We had some players crying every second day, and they didn't want to be at training. Some players really struggled with what top-level athletes go through. The pressure can get intense. It was a tough environment—cut-throat, especially if you were one of the younger players.

Most elite players back then were older, so as a younger player, I remember having to pick up all the balls after training, and I would know it if I accidentally kicked someone during training because I would get yelled at. It's a bit different these days because there are a lot more younger players in the team. As tough as it was, it made me more resilient and taught me you must earn respect from others, which is an important life lesson.

Did you move on from Brisbane Roar?
Emily: After a few years with Brisbane Roar, I made the Young Matildas' squad, and I scored a hat trick on my debut in a Young Matildas World Cup qualifier. We were losing 3-0 but ended up winning 4-3. It was an amazing feeling to have been able to do that, but we still didn't make the World Cup. Soon, I became too old for that squad, so that's when I started to push to make it into the national team.

What was it like trying to make it to the next level?
Emily: It wasn't easy. I found out recently a former Matilda turned television broadcaster used to ask the Matildas coach to select me for the Matildas' camp, but he insisted I wasn't ready.

While you were waiting for your big break, were you still playing with Brisbane Roar?
Emily: No, I wasn't. I wanted to go overseas, so I worked extremely hard to get into another club. Liverpool FC wanted to sign me, but there was a problem with the points system they have over there. To play in England, you have to achieve a certain number of points relating to how many minutes you play with your national team or club. That's why they have very good, experienced players over there. You either need to have played 70 per cent of your national team games or in the Champions League or won the league. The problem was I was still young, so I didn't have enough points yet.

Eventually, despite my lack of points, I got there, and I played for Liverpool FC.

What was that experience like?
Emily: I didn't really enjoy it. I had to drive a long way to get to training, and I wasn't

used to the cold weather. It was also the first time I had moved away from home, so I felt homesick.

Were you playing though?
Emily: Yes, I was. I was getting lots of game time. That wasn't the issue for me.

So, when did you eventually debut with the Matildas?
Emily: While I played with Liverpool FC, the Matildas coach selected me for the Matildas' squad. I debuted with Katrina Gorry in 2012 against Japan.

What was it like debuting with the Matildas?
Emily: I felt like it was a long time coming. I really had to work hard to earn it. I attended many camps before I debuted. It took years, but that just made it even more special when I finally got in.

Tell us about your time as a Matilda.
Emily: I became a regular starting eleven player, playing in the right-wing position. I was certain I would be selected for the squad to attend Cyprus for the World Cup, but when names were read out, mine wasn't called.

How did that make you feel?
Emily: I was shocked. I had just been 'chopped' from the Matildas' squad. It hurt. I remember thinking, *There goes my first World Cup opportunity.*

Did you ever find out why you weren't selected?
Emily: No, I didn't. Sometimes, there is no real reason. You just have to accept it.

Did you get back in?
Emily: The Olympics were coming up, and I had my sights set on that. I was in a good place, playing well, feeling fit and ready; however, the coach decided to pick another player over me.

Again, the feeling of disbelief came flooding back. It really knocked me down, and the self-doubt kicked in. I wasn't sure how to come back from that setback. It really hurt because I felt like I was so close.

Take us through that moment you were told you didn't make the squad.
Emily: I hated it. Those moments are always brutal. Each player gets called into a room individually where you are met by the coach and someone else. You never know what they are going to say, so it's always nerve-racking. On that occasion, I walked in,

I was told, "*Sorry, it's a 'no',*" and I was given the reason, which was they chose someone else over me, and they gave me the reasons why they chose the other player. Those moments are never easy for anyone.

For me, it was hard because I sacrificed so much, worked incredibly hard and did everything I could do to get selected, and it still wasn't enough. With that said, that's life. Football success is often based on someone's opinion at the time.

So, you missed the Olympics. Where did you go from there?
Emily: Soon afterwards, a new coach was assigned to the Matildas. I felt like I had been given a clean slate to prove myself again. He knew nothing about me, or women's football, but he was a great coach. From the get-go he really believed in me. He was tough, but honest. He demanded a lot more from me and helped me believe in myself again.

In what way was he honest?
Emily: He made it clear to me I had the attributes to go in a positive direction, or I could just as easily go in a negative direction. He made the players take ownership of their own future. He made it known the opportunity was there for the taking, if we showed him how much we wanted it. He selected solely on performance and the player's intention of giving everything to the team. He brought the same level of professionalism to the women's team that he provided the men's.

How did this mentality have an impact on your own performance?
Emily: His coaching style worked for me. I was consistently performing well, and I believe I was his number one pick for a very long time; so much so, it was because of him I got my first World Cup opportunity.

Wow. Tell us about your first FIFA Women's World Cup.
Emily: To be honest, before I had made the national team, I was so distraught from years of never 'making it' that I gave up on the idea. The second I gave up, opened my gym business, played with Brisbane Roar and started feeling happy, that's when I started playing well again. There was a real shift in my performance when I relaxed and stopped putting pressure on myself. Consequently, that's when I got my first call up for the Matildas. To this day, my partner reminds me not to think too far ahead, and to just get out there and enjoy myself. If I do that, everything else will just follow.

I was in a really good place. I was feeling great, like I was flying. In round one, we played against Italy, and I didn't play a single minute.

I remember panicking and thinking, *Maybe I'm not where I thought I was,* then we had to play and win against Brazil. It was the most important game for us. The coach came up to me and said, *"You know why you're playing this game, don't you?"* I replied, *"No, I didn't play the last game, so I'm a little bit worried."* He said, *"Well, you didn't play the first game, but you are playing this one. You are in the starting eleven; I'm putting my best team out there, and it's a 'must win' game. This is a big game for me, and you're playing, so if that doesn't tell you something, then I don't know what will."*

That was enough for me to realise my coach did believe in me. It enabled me to let go of not getting any time in the first game and focus on the job ahead. So many ups and downs, in terms of emotions, but the reality is, that's football.

How did you perform?
Emily: I was so nervous that I got sick. The stress, the heat and the anxiety of playing in my first World Cup game got to me, but thankfully, I did enough. I played seventy or eighty minutes, so I got through a fair chunk, and I figured if I was that bad, I would've come off at half time.

From that game onwards, I played consistently throughout the rest of the tournament.

There was one game though that I'll never forget. It was the game against Norway, which went to penalty shootouts. I knew I was in the coach's top three picks for penalty takers. He would always make me practise taking them under pressure at training to prepare me, and I never missed one. I became very confident in taking them; however, after Sam (Sam Kerr) missed hers, I had this awful feeling in the pit of my stomach, not because Sam missed but because the anxiety came flooding back. It got to me so much I didn't hit the ball the same way I usually would, and I missed.

Do you remember what that moment was like right before you took the penalty?
Emily: I would've been nervous, but on top of that, you feel a different type of pressure when you're next after someone has missed.

What was your reaction after you missed the penalty?
Emily: I'm surprised with the way I reacted. I was crying a lot, of course, but all I wanted to do when I got back to playing for my club was take another penalty to help me get past it. I took three penalties that season and scored all of them. In fact, I became the top goal scorer that year.

After the world knew I had missed my penalty in the World Cup, which prohibited the team from progressing from the quarter-finals, I came back with a vengeance and had a good season. I wanted to redeem myself, and I felt like I did.

That experience of missing that penalty in the World Cup motivated me to do better. Since then, I have always put my hand up to take a penalty, and to this day,

PART 3: GOING PRO

I haven't missed one, not even when I came up against Mackenzie Arnold. My experience in that World Cup led to a massive turning point in my career.

What was your next big move after the World Cup?
Emily: After the World Cup, Bayern Munich in Germany was interested in me. They are a big club in the Champions League with the best facilities in the world, so I signed a one-year deal with them.

You've travelled overseas a lot for football. Can you take us through all the clubs you went to up until Bayern Munich in Germany?
Emily: Overseas, I started off at Liverpool FC, then I went to Canada, then Japan, then Norway, then Sweden, and lastly, Bayern Munich. After Bayern Munich, I went to Aston Villa in England, but we'll talk more about that later.

I have been fortunate enough to play around the world and that was what I wanted. Football allowed me to experience different cultures and different styles of play.

Japan was challenging. No one spoke English. I was very isolated and had insomnia for a month. I only slept three hours a day. It was crazy. I can't believe I got through that. Despite that, I was still happy there.

Bayern Munich had its own set of challenges for me. Their coaching style was very different to what I was used to.

I am the type of person who likes to push myself beyond my comfort zone, to test myself beyond my perceived limits, to see how I cope.

Tell us more about your time at Bayern Munich.
Emily: We had eighteen national team players, so each week someone was missing from the team. That was fortunate for me because it meant I never missed out on making the squad, except for once, when I went away for a Matildas' camp. When I got back, they told me they couldn't put me on the team that week because I had been away.

My time there was great, especially given I was able to play in the Champions League.

What came next?
Emily: I got selected for the Olympics. My first Olympics! The Matildas coach at this time gave me an immense amount of game time, but before long, I felt things shifting and began to lose belief in myself again. I got inside my own head and wondered if perhaps I wasn't good enough anymore. It started to feel like I was at a loss, and my performance declined too. These times can have a massive impact on your mental health. I was effectively dropped. I was so disappointed.

Tell us about your time at Aston Villa.
Emily: Aston Villa was the only club I signed a two-year deal with.

I had a great first season with them. I played every single minute of every single game. In my second year, I experienced two calf tears and a bad tackle on my ankle which consequently led to missing the 2023 FIFA Women's World Cup.

That must have been devastating. Tell us about that.
Emily: I should have recovered from the ankle injury well before the World Cup, but so much went wrong during the rehabilitation stage. I couldn't run properly. I couldn't even put my football boot on. Despite that, I was willing to run through a brick wall to make that squad, so I trained during the first week of the Matildas' camp while enduring an incredible amount of pain. I kept up with the fittest of players, pushed myself to another level I didn't even know I was capable of. The desire I had to be selected was like nothing I had ever felt before.

I still remember the day I was in Germany and running in a park with some friends, when it was announced Australia had won the bid to host the 2023 FIFA Women's World Cup. I started crying because I couldn't believe it. I couldn't believe that, in my lifetime, I was possibly going to play in a World Cup at home. From then on, I was determined to be part of that once-in-a-lifetime opportunity. The one being played at home. My home. Australia.

I have a high pain threshold and a lot of grit. I think that's something I bring to a team, and I think it's important to have at least one person like that because it's that mentality that can help carry a squad through.

How did you cope when you weren't selected?
Emily: To be honest, I still cry about it to this day. That was the toughest *'no'* I have ever heard. Maybe this is a bit selfish of me to say, but I know I could have given something to the team, even if it was off the pitch.

What do you think you could've brought to the team off the pitch?
Emily: It can be a lonely and selfish game at the top. It's hard to get in there, but it's even harder to stay. Naturally, everyone must put themselves first. However, throughout my career, I've always put my feelings aside to lift others up, even if they were taking my position and I was sitting on the bench. It's the innate, pure love of the game that I have which allows me to lift others, even at my own expense. At the very least, I know I could've offered my unconditional support to the 2023 World Cup squad.

How were you told 'No'?
Emily: I attended the first three weeks of the pre-World Cup Matildas' camp, then after

PART 3: GOING PRO

that, we were due to attend a second three-week block. I was told I wasn't required to attend the second block, and I wasn't even allowed to attend training.

I felt like I went from being part of a family to nobody overnight. I felt like my whole world had just been turned upside down.

How did the rest of the squad react?
Emily: The day I said goodbye and good luck to the girls was hard. Everyone was crying. Most of us have been on the same journey for approximately ten years. We'd been through many milestones together. We truly felt like a family. I believe they felt the devastation for me, and I would've felt the same if it was one of them.

How did you pick yourself up after this setback?
Emily: This was the first time I felt unsure if I could come back from such a setback.

It brought Chloe Logarzo and me closer because we were going through the same thing together. Having said that, I really wanted Chloe to get selected and go because then at least one of us would've been there.

I was asked to support the Matildas through a broadcasting opportunity with Chloe. While this was a great distraction, not many people will understand how hard that was for both of us. It all looks glamorous on TV, but deep down, talking about the team and being on the sidelines with a microphone when you're usually the one running on the pitch was difficult. The further the Matildas went in the tournament, the more I wished I was there being part of it all. The world witnessed the history they were making. Regardless, I'm incredibly proud of the team and what they did for women's football.

In the end, I had to take it in stride and handle it the best way I could. I know a World Cup at home will never happen again. That's a fact, and I have to live with that.

In terms of your playing career post-World Cup, what did you do?
Emily: Coming off the missed World Cup, I signed with Melbourne Victory. They took a risk on me because I failed the medical. I still couldn't run. There was still something wrong with my ankle, but I was given an injection and walked pain-free for the first time in six months. I had the injection another two times, and my ankle still wasn't 100 per cent, but I began training and running. Eight months following my injury, I played my first game with Melbourne Victory.

I really like my current coach. I think he's fair, and I was clear with him from the beginning when I said to him, *"If I deserve to play, play me. If I'm not performing, bench me."* I don't want young players coming through thinking Matildas are entitled to everything.

How did your first season at Melbourne Victory play out?
Emily: In terms of the ankle injury, it felt a little bit weird in the first game, but to make matters worse, I tore my calf muscle during the second game.

Do you think this is your body telling you to slow down?
Emily: I don't think so because I feel great, and I don't want to believe that. I think it's the mental stress of the year that had passed leading to further injuries. I believe stress can affect you physically too.

The funny thing is, the day I tore my calf, I was out on the pitch having fun again. I got close to scoring two goals, and I had an assist. I think that's the sole reason I decided not to hang up my boots.

I found my love for the game again, in those five minutes!

How long were you out for due to this new injury?
Emily: I was out for another eight weeks.

Now, in my mind, I'm focusing purely on getting back out there and doing what I love, just praying and hoping that all the rewards will follow. I'm trying to stay in the present. Melbourne Victory values and cares about me right now, so that's who I want to give my energy to.

What would you say to the young kids playing today?
Emily: The reality is the rollercoaster of emotions is intense in elite football. The ups and downs are all part of the journey. Someone can be the coach's favourite one day, and then out the next. You can have an injury setting you back, but someone else's injury can give you your break. You can be out quickly, but you can get back in just as quickly. You must always stay ready so when your chance comes, you can take it.

Aspiring athletes have got to have that 'never-give-up' mentality. I could've quit one thousand times, but I didn't. One of the biggest takeaways for the young kids reading my story is I was told *'no'* a lot at the start when I wasn't professional, then when I became professional, I was still being told *'no'.* Yet here I am today. You will be told *'no'* again and again. Be prepared for that. Be resilient.

If I had to do it all again, I wouldn't change anything. Without my experiences, I wouldn't be the player I am today and have a strong level of resilience. This important life skill will transfer into other parts of my life, including what I choose to do after football.

Another thing I would like to remind kids is I knew I wasn't talented when I was young. I did not have skill. Sometimes, I was embarrassed by some of the mistakes I'd make on the pitch; however, I was so dedicated I did whatever it took. I was the first to arrive at training and the last to leave. I would practise hundreds of free kicks, do extra

PART 3: GOING PRO

training with boys, even train at my local park with boys. There wasn't a day that went by (that) I did not train. Sometimes I would even train two or three times in one day, including in my own backyard. I lived and breathed it because I knew that if I wanted any chance of being a professional, I had to work very hard. Having said that, practising football didn't feel like a chore. It was my lifestyle and my way of having fun. I knew I wasn't one of those gifted kids in terms of technical ability, but I had a lot of motivation and competitiveness.

There are a lot of kids these days trying to make it into certain teams, but I encourage them to ask themselves, *"If I was the coach, would I pick me? Have I worked hard? Do I really want it?"* If you answer yes and you still don't get selected, that's okay. Maybe you just aren't ready yet. Keep working hard and have fun with it.

What advice would you give to kids who are highly motivated to succeed?
Emily: Shift the post from time to time. Step outside of your comfort zone because when you do, that's when you realise how much further your boundaries and abilities extend. Make sacrifices like moving and playing overseas. When I played in England, many of my teammates were national team players from around the world. Every training session was a matter of 'kill it' or 'be killed'. Every game is the hardest game of my life. I had to earn my jersey to play each week. That experience pushed me to get better.

What advice would you give to kids who are truly trying but are still struggling to succeed as footballers?
Emily: If you set your mind on something and you don't accomplish it, it doesn't matter. When one door closes another one opens. I could easily have decided to stay home by myself when I wasn't selected for the 2023 World Cup. Instead, as hard as it was, I took the broadcasting opportunity. As a result, I met many more people and attended more public speaking events. Be open to other opportunities because you never know what can come from it.

When you get told *'no'* and you're given another opportunity, take it.

How can older kids or young adults find the time to prepare for a life outside of football when they are pursuing a football career?
Emily: Everyone has time if they want to make the time. Yes, it can be exhausting, but you can always find a pocket of time if you want something bad enough.

MAKING IT...OR NOT

Callum Nicholas

"The difference between men playing in the semi-pro league and playing academy football is that, when you win, it means more to semi-pro players ... This was the year I got my love back for football, and I wasn't playing in the highest league!"

You had a successful season in the U18 squad at Liverpool FC, even got an opportunity to train and play with the first team. The next step was obviously to get your first professional contract. How did your chase for that contract start?

Callum: After my first season with the U18 team, I became one of the older players on the team. Our first game of the season was against Manchester City. I played in the midfield with Trent Alexander-Arnold and Herbie Kane. During the game, I started to get pain in my knee, and I had to get scans done. Turned out, I needed to have surgery.

I was devastated because this was the year I had to do well to get a professional contract.

I had the surgery and was out for six months.

Did you struggle to get back to the same level following the surgery?
Callum: Not really, because I started training every day, and the physiotherapist knew what to do to help rebuild my strength again.

I got fit, and I started doing well again. I was back. So much so that the academy manager spoke to me and said, *"Don't be the 'nearly man'. You are so close!"* I played consistently well for two months when I started to get pain in my groin, and it wouldn't go away. I ended up having to go to the hospital.

I was sent to get an injection in my hip. If I could run after having the injection, then it would mean I would need surgery. That's how they test for the injury I had. Jordan Henderson was at the hospital that day for something else, and I told him about it. He wished me luck, and I went off to get my injection. I went for a run afterwards, and the pain had completely gone. So, the same year I had my knee surgery, I also had hip surgery, and that was a vital year when it was important for me to stay fit and perform!

I had the surgery, and the surgeon said to me I had a 50 per cent chance of playing again.

What was wrong with the hip?
Callum: The joints on the hip are supposed to glide. Mine were clutching due to wear and tear. Given it's the hip, it's a bit dangerous. This is why I needed to undergo surgery.

PART 3: GOING PRO

How did the surgery go?
Callum: The surgery went well, but I was out for seven to eight months.

Do you think the injuries could have been caused by 'wear and tear' from having a hectic training schedule from such a young age?
Callum: Possibly. The fact that I had 'wear and tear' provided no protection for the movements I made, which ultimately led to the injury.

Did you get a professional contract?
Callum: In that vital year, when coaches decide if you're going to get a professional contract, I only played for two months, at most.

I was in the physiotherapy room one day, and I was told management wanted to speak to me. They told me they weren't going to give me a professional contract, but they would provide me with all the rehabilitation my body needed at that time, even if it continued into the following season. They also told me I wasn't going to get paid anymore. I was gutted because I couldn't afford to do that.

At the very least, I thought I would be able to get fit again and get some training in before I could go and trial at other clubs, but due to the law, I couldn't even train with them.

So, I had been injured for six months and then another eight months. Without having trained in a long time, I had to start trialling at other clubs. It was a nightmare.

Did you manage to trial elsewhere, and if so, where?
Callum: Yes, first I went to Wigan Athletic FC. They are a club in the Championship League. I started training, but I couldn't turn or do much with my body. I struggled. I didn't go back because I couldn't perform and knew I wasn't going to get offered a contract while I was in poor condition.

What did you do instead?
Callum: All I needed was to train somewhere. I ended up going to Burnley FC. Burnley agreed to give me a length of time to get my sharpness and flexibility back. I was happy with this because I had quite a few friends there too. I started doing well again, played a few games, and my manager told me it was likely I was going to get signed. By then, I was eighteen years old.

Unfortunately, the manager at the time didn't want to sign me. He felt I was too small for the midfield. I ended up having to leave Burnley FC. By this stage it was September, and the season had started in August, so a month went by where I didn't play anywhere. Consequently, I lost my fitness again.

How did you push through such a challenging time when you knew time was running out?

Callum: I went to a field every day and did a lot of running. I was going to the gym every day as well. I wouldn't give up, but it was a depressing time for me.

Did you eventually play in a team again?

Callum: I ended up signing for my local, non-league team called FC United. It's a club formed by all the Manchester United fans. They had quite a large fan base. Sometimes they had three to four thousand fans at a game, and I got paid to play with them.

What was your experience with FC United like?

Callum: While I was playing there, I got a trial with Cardiff City. I went there, did well and they offered me a professional contract. One night before a game against Arsenal, I received a phone call from Cardiff City advising me they couldn't sign me because I played a competitive game for FC United, and I had to wait until January (the transfer window). It was only October. I was shocked and incredibly upset because I was never informed about this clause when I signed with FC United.

Did you go to Cardiff City in January?

Callum: By January, Cardiff City had already got someone else in, so that opportunity was no longer available, and by this stage, I had left FC United too.

That's such a shame for you. What did you do?

Callum: By then I hadn't played in a professional environment for one and a half years. I went to Watford FC. One of the U23 coaches wanted to sign me, but the other one didn't. Watford FC did offer me a place to stay and money for petrol, but no income. I couldn't afford to accept that.

How tough was that time for you?

Callum: Very tough. Agents were trying to sort things out for me, but the season had already started, so clubs were no longer interested. At that point, I wasn't sure I wanted to keep chasing it anymore. I went an entire season without playing.

So, what else did you do during that season you missed?

Callum: I stayed home and didn't do much at all. I felt very defeated. When I got my first injury at seventeen, I started gambling to numb the hurt and lost lots of money. When Watford FC told me they would only be willing to offer me a place to stay and money for petrol, I went home and lost money to gambling again, money I didn't have. I didn't realise it at the time, but I resorted to unhealthy habits to cope with my situation.

PART 3: GOING PRO

Thankfully, I knew I was dealing with the stress in an unhealthy way, so I banned myself from gambling. I deleted all the apps off my phone. I acknowledge I am one of the lucky ones who didn't continue down the dangerous path of gambling addiction.

Did you eventually go back to football?
Callum: While I was at home wondering what to do next, one of my friends from school asked me to play for his team, Erling FC. It's a local, non-league, semi-professional team. He told me I would earn some money playing with them too. I hadn't played in a year. Nonetheless, I went, and I really enjoyed it.

What did you enjoy about it?
Callum: The team was made up of a group of local lads, and it was very competitive, more competitive than any other league I had ever played in before. I played against grown men. I was twenty years old, and it was the most fun I ever had playing football! The team did well that year too. We ended up doing so well, we played in the FA Cup on TV.

That's exciting. Can you tell us a little bit about what it's like playing in this league?
Callum: The difference between men playing in the semi-pro league and playing academy football is that, when you win, it means more to semi-pro players. When they win, they get paid a bit more, which is important, because a lot of them have families to feed. This was the year I got my love back for football, and I wasn't playing in the highest league!

Did you have to get another job, or was it enough money just playing for this team?
Callum: I was only getting paid a little bit, so I needed another job. My dad had a job looking after disabled adults at the time. I started working as a support worker with him and did that for four years before I moved to Australia. I had a friend who was playing for Nottingham Forest FC, and when he stopped playing, he worked with us too.

What was it like working in something other than in football?
Callum: I liked the job. I got a sense of satisfaction from doing it. It felt good to help others. On top of that, the hours of work were flexible, so if I needed to take time off for football, I was able to do that. It was during this time I started studying a university degree through the Professional Football Association (PFA) too.

MAKING IT...OR NOT

Diogo Ferreira

"I would sit on the sideline thinking, What's going on here? *It felt like I had gone to the bottom of the barrel. Fast forward a bit, and I was the first one to be offered a professional contract. It's important to have resilience to push through the difficult times."*

At what point did you know football was going to be your career?
Diogo: I think it was when I was overseas in Portugal the first time.

When did you go pro, and how did it come about?
Diogo: I came back to Australia at eighteen years old, when the A-League had just started. I had this vision of coming back to Australia, playing in the A-League and getting selected for the Australian Olympic team for my age group. That was my new goal. I had the mentality that if I can't make it in the A-League, then I'm never going to make it in Europe, so it became my ultimate test.

No one knew who I was because there was no information on the internet regarding every player around the world like there is now.

I signed with the Green Gully FC Senior NPL team in Melbourne, and it was a good team with some really good players. I had this preconceived idea that, coming from Portugal, I would go straight into the A-League, but that wasn't the case. I had to remain patient and follow the steps to prove myself first.

Luckily, I was noticed, and from there, I moved to Melbourne Victory Youth Team. During my first season with Melbourne Victory Youth Team, I was the first person to be selected from my group to train with the senior team. It felt rewarding to be selected, but deep down I also felt like I was ready. As the season went on, everyone started getting chosen to train with the senior team, and sometimes when there was a game, others would be chosen to play before me. I would sit on the sideline thinking, *What's going on here?* It felt like I had gone to the bottom of the barrel. Fast forward a bit and I was the first one to be offered a professional contract. It's important to have resilience to push through the difficult times.

In terms of emotions, there are a lot of ups and downs.

What were some of the moments of elation you experienced?
Diogo: When I went to Melbourne Victory, I remember scoring against Wellington Phoenix at AAMI Park in Melbourne. I played as a defender, so it's not like I was able to score all the time. I remember the next day I was featured on the back of the Herald

PART 3: GOING PRO

Sun. That was special. I also remember being away for a month with the U23 Australian National Team, and when I got back, I still made the starting eleven straight away. My career was on the rise at that time, and I was only twenty. I also remember playing a good game against Sydney FC.

What struggles and setbacks did you experience during your time playing as a professional?

Diogo: I had a very well-known senior coach at Melbourne Victory who didn't really want me to stay, but through persistence and hard work, I managed to prove him wrong and ended up playing every game that season. By the end of the season, he wanted to keep me on the team, but unfortunately, due to signed commitments with other players, there was no space left for me. He had the task of telling me he couldn't keep me anymore, despite telling my agent he was. He was very honest at the time, and I acknowledge it would've been difficult for him to have that conversation, but I was hurt. Back then I felt I didn't deserve it because I was a nice guy, got along with all my teammates, worked hard and performed consistently.

However, because of this decision, I moved to Brisbane Roar where I won my only championship. It was the most enjoyable year of my professional career!

Moving to Brisbane did mean moving away from my family again. This was something I was used to, but at this stage, I was dating too. My partner would travel back and forth to see me, which wasn't easy for her. We spent a lot of money on flights!

Professional football players must put their careers first, and I was lucky enough to have a partner who understood and supported me through that. She still does! I would've loved for her to have moved with me, and some elite athletes do ask this of their partners, but I always felt it would be unfair to ask her to move for me to chase my dream. I left it to her to decide if she wanted to do that, and one year later, she did. She moved to Perth when I moved to Perth Glory.

What was your lifestyle like as a professional player?

Diogo: During my time as a professional player, more specifically, during my time at Perth Glory, I had a luxury life in terms of lifestyle. I played football for a career, went to the beach after training and spent time with my partner. However, it was nothing like what you see in the media. I wasn't driving around in a Ferrari or living in a mansion. We were living in an apartment. It had a pool, which was nice. One day, we wondered why no one was in the pool, only to realise it's because everyone else was at work. That was good, but I can't recall ever having a weekend to myself. That never existed. Not even now.

Was football your only source of income, or did you have another job?
Diogo: While I was at Melbourne Victory, I owned two Kelly Sports franchises to help earn some extra money. While I was with Perth Glory, I worked for Kelly Sports as a second job. My partner got a job in Perth too. I remember paying $500 per week in rent for a one-bedroom apartment because it was during a time when there was a boom in the mining industry, so rent in Perth was very expensive.

An average wage in the men's A-League allows you to survive and live comfortably, but it's important for kids to know there's a short lifespan in football. If you get an injury, you're done. Your body might only allow you to play until the age of thirty-two. Everyone else who is earning the same as you at thirty-two will probably keep getting more and more as their careers continue to grow, while you will have to start from scratch again. Playing professional football certainly doesn't mean you will live a luxurious and rich life.

Was there financial uncertainty, and how did you cope with that?
Diogo: I only ever had a two-year contract on two occasions throughout my entire professional career. Prior to that, I lived one year at a time without knowing if my contract was going to be renewed for another year. I had no idea where my source of income was going to come from or how much it was going to be from one season to the next. This was stressful, especially when I had to move my entire life to wherever my club was and even more stressful when my partner had to move her life too.

Admittedly, you feel good during pre-season when you first sign your new deal, but it's only four months later when negotiations for the following year commence, and the feeling of uncertainty creeps in again. The pressures and stress of that are hard. It's important to have something to fall back on, especially if you have a family.

What was your relationship like with the other players?
Diogo: In terms of relationships with teammates, I'm the type of person who always got along with everyone. Of course, there were clique groups, but I chose to move around and speak to everyone. I found myself being particularly supportive towards overseas players because I could speak Spanish, which is where a lot of them came from. I enjoyed a bit of camaraderie and playing pranks on the other players, like the time I put Glad Wrap around one of my teammate's cars. With that said, you form these close relationships with your teammates while you're playing together. You see each other nearly every day, you have a lot in common, you travel together, but it's like you form no emotional connection because you know next year they're going somewhere else, and I might be going somewhere else too. You might bump into them one day or you might not, but you move on and make new friends. That's just the industry.

PART 3: GOING PRO

How good are clubs in providing support to professional players?
Diogo: It's much better now. Support from clubs has come a long way. Clubs have a welfare manager to support players and there's also the Professional Football Association (PFA). The PFA even helped me when I moved to Asia. They helped me get paid and reviewed my contracts. They can provide legal, financial and contract advice and assistance, and they also provide free sports psychologist sessions. Most players see a sports psychologist these days as they understand a healthy mind plays a big part in their performance. On top of that, seeing a sports psychologist is considered a 'cool' thing amongst the players. It's much more accepted now. I feel that if you don't use the resources available to you, it's because you don't want to use them.

When I was fifteen and moved to Portugal, I had to sit with a sports psychologist upon arrival. They were very much ahead of the game in terms of mental health. I still have the booklet I was given which addresses things like how to deal with pressure and has all sorts of tips on how to stay mentally healthy. This did not exist in Australia nineteen years ago.

Do clubs encourage players to do further studies like TAFE or university courses?
Diogo: In terms of assisting with a career or education outside of football, I believe that if you're not studying, it's because you don't want to. The club's welfare manager and the PFA can assist players with this. The PFA provides financial assistance towards various courses as well. They can certainly pay for things like a Cert III or IV in fitness or a coaching course, just to name a few. The majority of players are doing something on the side because they understand a football career is short-lived.

The times in my career when I performed well, I had a distraction from football. There was a time when I was training that I would come home and play *FIFA* on the PlayStation or watch football games. One day, I decided to stop playing *FIFA* and watching games. I needed to find a healthy balance. Funnily enough, a lot of people ask me who I follow in the Premier League. I don't follow anyone. I watch games sometimes, but I don't follow anyone because I don't want to be tempted to watch more games. I need to switch off from football sometimes. It's important. I always give this example to the kids I train now, who are coming through the academy system.

You need to have something outside of football. Firstly, for your future but also for your wellbeing. Otherwise, it becomes too overwhelming, and you end up not performing well because it's all you can think about.

At what point did football stop being fun?
Diogo: Football stopped being fun when I left Brisbane Roar and went to Perth Glory. I had some ups and downs there. I started to question and doubt my professional performance. Eventually, I got to a point where I was desperate for a change, and

that's when I moved to Asia.

Initially, Asia gave me the spark and excitement I needed because it was somewhere new, and I loved travelling, until I realised Asia was a very different world, and much like Portugal, very cutthroat. You may only have three foreigners on your team, but if the team played badly, it was always the foreigners' fault, even if the foreigners played well. I came onto a pitch in Malaysia once, and even though I had been playing well, a sign read *'Diogo is a Parasite'.* I was shocked, but I also laughed. I understood I was being targeted because I was a foreigner, and as a foreigner, I was probably being paid more. That didn't sit well with them.

I spent four years in Asia playing for clubs in Indonesia, Malaysia, India and Japan. I feel grateful football allowed me and my partner to visit different countries and experience different cultures. We were able to explore the world. In bad times when a club wanted to drop me, I used to think *I'm just going to stay here until you give me what I'm owed and enjoy the culture while I can.* That was always the upside during difficult or sad times.

Do you think you 'made it'?
Diogo: If I'm going to be honest, I feel like I didn't 'make it'. I don't like saying that because some kids would kill to do what I have done, like score goals in front of fans, hear the chant of your name coming from stadium seats or walk out to sixty thousand fans in the first eleven for a derby. I just feel, for all the hard work I put in, I didn't 'make it'.

My partner thinks I'm crazy when I tell her that. Over time she has helped me realise my football career as a player was my apprenticeship for my coaching job now. I couldn't agree more.

Part 4:
Life After Football

Every footballer faces an inevitable truth: their career will end one day.

A professional football career is not a given. It is tough to attain and will end at some point, so it's essential to have a back-up plan. It's short-lived because of the athletic demands of the game and the number of players competing for spots. In some unfortunate circumstances, a player's time can come to an unexpected and abrupt end, as an injury may take that athlete out of the running.

Thankfully, all the players interviewed for this book prove that a happy, fulfilling life after football is possible and that dreams and aspirations off the field exist. The Taranto girls are well-established educators, already successfully balancing two careers. As the saying goes, where there's a will, there's a way.

Life After Football Stats

- 1,715,441 and growing = number of football players in Australia
- Mid to late 20s—the age football players typically reach their peak
- 35 years—the average age of retirement from football
- Other career paths within the football industry:
    - Coaching and player development
    - Broadcasting, media and technology
    - Business and sales
    - Education
    - Community
    - Governance
    - Health

PART 4: LIFE AFTER FOOTBALL

Joshua Risdon

What do you think your legacy is now?
Josh: During the time I saw a sports psychologist, I realised one of the things I searched for was my purpose in life and meaning. As I'm getting older, I'm realising there is so much more to life than football. It's about doing what you feel is your purpose.

I think this book is amazing and there needs to be more of it because I had no idea going into it what the journey was truly like, and I wish I did. I bottled up a lot of emotions and thought it was normal. Now, I want to help by giving any advice I can to prepare the next generation coming through the system. I want to tell them the pressures they put on themselves aren't real, and everyone just wants to see them be happy and do well.

Inevitably, there are many pressures that come with being an elite football player, and there are different types of challenges too. There are injuries, deselections and many more. The game is better now because there's more support through clubs who have sports psychologists, and it's extremely important to seek that help if you think you need it. What I've noticed is that when I'm in a better headspace, I'm playing a lot better too.

What do you think is next for you?
Josh: I'm still playing, but I'm also studying to be a PE teacher. I feel this could be my way of giving back and being a great support to young kids who might want to pursue a sport professionally.

Chloe Logarzo

What are your plans moving forward?
Chloe: The whole reason I play football is because I want to play for my national team, and I haven't given up on that yet.

I also enjoy playing in the domestic league, but like any job, you experience ups and downs. If I'm having a great season, I love it. If I'm having a bad season, I feel down.

The other thing to factor in, too, is the domestic-league wage isn't great for women yet. Some of the players on our national team get paid well, while many others are still on a minimum wage, which is only enough to just get by. For six years, I was getting paid to play domestically and getting paid for being in the national team squad. Now, I'm only on a domestic-league wage. I have a house mortgage, and for the first time in eight years, when this season is over, I may not have an income. It's terrifying, especially now that I am twenty-nine years old.

Is there another career path you might like to pursue once you hang up your boots?
Chloe: Fellow Matilda, Emily Gielnik, and I have developed a clinic for young girls called 'Future Baller'. It's new, but we have big plans for that.

In terms of a full-time career outside of football, I would love to work for a company called 'Stryker'. It's a technology company that builds medical devices. When I had my ACL injury, Stryker put devices in my knee. I have known about the company for many years because one of my housemates in Kansas City worked for them, and they like engaging athletes.

I think it would be rewarding to be able to promote and sell their devices, given how much they have helped me. I've always loved learning about anatomy too. It's a topic that intrigues me, so the idea of helping surgeons insert devices into body parts like knees and ankles to help others really excites me.

The biggest thing worrying me about leaving football is the level of competitiveness, particularly in medical sales. I may be at a disadvantage because I am not a 'normal' person coming from a 'normal' background, and I don't have any experience yet. I understand I need to start from scratch again and be willing to learn, otherwise I could lose control over my future.

PART 4: LIFE AFTER FOOTBALL

Emily Gielnik

You mentioned earlier you owned a gym. Tell us about that.
Emily: Yes, I did. I had my own gym. It was large. We offered strength and conditioning classes, and I worked with men's football teams as well. I loved it!

What are your plans after football?
Emily: As Chloe mentioned, we have created the 'Future Baller' clinic together. This isn't your ordinary clinic. It's very personalised. Drills are created with specific positions in mind, and we have very good coaches. It'll run for five hours, in two locations, Melbourne and Sydney. We want the girls who attend this clinic to develop technically, but we also want to be transparent about what it takes to 'make it'. We want to help them develop the right mindset and mentality too.

This clinic is a stepping stone for something greater that we want to pursue in the future, which includes telling our stories like we have in this book, developing podcasts, and other things along those lines.

MAKING IT...OR NOT

Callum Nicholas

Do you feel clubs do enough to support players during career transitions and other difficult times in football?
Callum: With Liverpool FC, I would say they were quite good. They had a guy named Phil Roscoe who was the Head of Welfare. I used to receive a text message from him every six months asking if I needed anything. I would also get an email from him every month with updates on what was happening at the club and a separate email detailing what the PFA could offer players like me. I know that if I wanted to go back to Liverpool FC and help coach young kids, he would probably have said yes to that. He's left Liverpool FC now, but when he was still there, I would still get regular communication from him. He was great.

Is coaching something that interests you for the future?
Callum: I don't think so.

What can the PFA provide you with?
Callum: Once you are a PFA member, you are a member for life. It's an association just for footballers. Professional players pay a fee every year. If you're not at a club anymore, you don't pay the yearly fee, but you are still a member. It's funded by the players and the Football Association (FA). If someone is struggling for money or in any other way, they will help find a way to support them.

Things didn't work out the way you had hoped or planned, and you had already dedicated your entire life to football because the industry requires that of you. What can players do once football is no longer an option?
Callum: That's what I found the hardest, thinking, *What do I do now?* Growing up I was seen as the boy who played football and likely to 'make it' to all my friends and family. Now, I feel I need to be smart about what job I choose to avoid being judged. I don't want people to think *What happened to him?* That's another reason I was grateful for the job I had with my dad. I didn't mind people knowing what happened to me, but in that job, I was away from any potential judgement.

What made you start a university degree?
Callum: One of my friends was doing the journalism and broadcasting degree through the PFA and recommended it to me. I understand having a university degree can open many doors in the future, so I decided to do it.

PART 4: LIFE AFTER FOOTBALL

Did you have to pay for your degree?
Callum: The PFA paid for most of it. They even gave me extra money to pay for materials such as a laptop, books and anything else I needed to complete the course.

Did you enjoy doing it?
Callum: It was okay. The course had to be completed remotely because a lot of the players doing the course were either still playing or working. During the course, you only have two weeks where you go to the university and meet with your classmates, and in those two weeks, we did practical assessments, such as creating recordings.

When did you graduate?
Callum: I graduated at the end of 2023. I went back home to the UK for my graduation and celebrated with my family. While I was there, I met a guy who has his own podcast now, after completing the same degree. His agent funded it, and he's doing well.

Congratulations on your graduation. What are your future career plans?
Callum: I would like to do something in the football industry, but I also need a decent income, so I'm not sure at this stage. What I do know though is now that I am a university graduate my options have opened.

Have you hung up your boots, or are you still playing now?
Callum: I am still playing. I'm currently playing for a semi-professional team in Australia. I have accepted I'm never going to make it to the highest level, and I'm okay with that.

What made you come to Australia?
Callum: I came to Australia because my life in the UK became a bit repetitive, which started to bore me. A few of my friends made the decision to come to Australia, so I decided to come too. I like it a lot. I'm having a great time. To be fair, the money you can earn here is a lot better than what you can make in England too. That's made me want to stay.

Do you have any regrets?
Callum: Sometimes I think I could have made better decisions or done things better. Even just the little things like being less shy as a kid and not being too scared to approach my coaches to find out what I could be doing better. In the end, though, it was ultimately my injuries preventing me from making it to the highest level, and that's something that's out of my control. I know some may say it's easy to blame injuries, but it all happened at such a vital time, and I was never the same after.

Diogo Ferreira

What are you doing now?

Diogo: I'm coaching, and I love it. I always knew I was going to be a better coach than I was a player. I just knew it. I was born to coach. When I was a kid, my dad and I would go to a game, and we would choose a player and study him the whole game. I would get a piece of paper and move away from my dad, take notes, and at the end of the game, go back to my dad and see if I got the same statistics as him. I was only thirteen years old.

I've been through all the highs and lows as a player, which I feel has made me a better coach. I can bring a level of understanding to the players that they may need. For example, I was never the best player on the team, so I know how all the mediocre players feel. I'm using my experiences to help me and those I'm coaching.

I always said that as a coach, one of the most important things for me is to always be honest with the players. I don't want any player to ever turn around and say I wasn't true to my word because I know what it feels like to not have that. Transparency is important to me.

I also get to help young kids in my skill development centre, which I love. I love watching them grow, seeing them get better, and I enjoy watching them bond with each other too. I don't really care whether they make it or not, so long as I see them getting better and enjoying it. I see what I've built there, and I feel proud. Parents come with smiles on their faces. Parents are happy. Kids are happy. Kids are sticking around even when they have finished their sessions. It's a bit like a family.

I feel I worked incredibly hard as a football player. So hard. I feel like I should've been the best player in the world, but now I believe that as a coach. The funny thing is I never said I was a good player when I was playing; however, as a coach, I can acknowledge I'm a good coach. I'm in a good place now, and this is the most enjoyable time in my football career—right now, as a coach!

The Parents' Role

(with a little advice for coaches too)

Players as young as eight fight each year during a trial period to keep their spot in their football team for the following season. They have formed friendships, and let's be honest, so have the parents. Therefore, it can be hard to accept when your child is dropped from the team for reasons parents don't always agree with or find difficult to accept.

Parents are often left with the task of lifting their children's spirits and providing a solution to help them overcome this situation. They find themselves trying to teach their children to work hard and reach for the stars and, at the same time, be realistic without sending the message to give up. It's a tough balancing act.

This book helps your child understand that it's never a straight line to the top, and even the most successful players in the world have encountered setbacks. It's a normal part of the process. However, with hard work and an understanding of what the real journey looks like, aspiring athletes will be much better equipped to navigate the difficult times.

The following chapter provides you, the parent, with a better understanding of how to best support your child when times get tough. The players, including a player who became a professional coach, provide advice based on what worked and didn't work for them. Afterwards, psychologist Lara Faga offers valuable advice some of you may wish you had received sooner.

THE PARENTS' ROLE

Player Viewpoints

What have you seen parents do today that makes you cringe?
Adriana: Parents are getting too involved. Helicopter parenting is a big issue. The other thing is coaching from the sidelines. It shouldn't happen. Parents need to respect the coach and what they are saying, even if it isn't always the right decision. If you must approach the coach, do so respectfully. If your child is not getting game time, especially at a senior level, that doesn't mean you can question the coach. Ask your child to approach the coach and seek advice on what they could work on to increase their chances first.

Melissa: Another thing we see parents do is tell their kids they are better than what they really are. Saying things like *"You're the best on the pitch"* isn't a good idea. Be supportive but be honest. It's all about trying to find the right balance. Let them live out their journey, their way. Support and give them feedback, but don't lift them too high or put them down too much.

Diogo: I see so many things parents do that makes me cringe. I don't even know where to start. Sadly, a common one is parents trying to live their dream through their kids. I see parents pushing their kids way too much when their kids are only six, seven or eight years old. I get calls from parents of young children worrying about their child's football career. They ask me what their next move should be. Which clubs should they take them to? I often respond with *"Just let the kid have fun!"* Let them enjoy it while they can.

There's so much time later if, or when, they get to a professional level. If there are two teams, and one team is much better, but your child is having the best time playing with the team that's not so good, go to the one that's not so good. I acknowledge that at some point you need to think about the future so that they don't regress, but not at such an early age.

What would you say to parents who might be a bit pushy?
Chloe: Know when it's the right time to push and when to nurture your child. Finding that balance is so important. You want to help them find and maintain their drive and desire without forcing it upon them, otherwise they might quit.

Diogo: My parents never pushed me. I can count on one hand how many times my dad would take me to the park because he got home late from work. He never took me to extra skills training or academy training either. He couldn't.

I remember once a former overseas player, who is now a well-known overseas senior coach, organised a local Saturday training session. My dad knew him, so after showing my interest, my dad agreed to take me to this because he had Saturdays off.

Had he been working, and had I not had the passion, he wouldn't have taken me to that. It was always me pushing my parents.

Callum: Looking back, I like how my dad pushed me a bit when I was young. If he didn't, maybe I wouldn't have pushed myself. There were times when I played badly, and I would think to myself *I can't let my dad see me playing like this!* That would push me to turn my game around and start playing better. He was never on the sidelines shouting though. He would talk to me about my performance in private afterwards.

If parents understand football, then it's acceptable to push a little bit, but I've noticed a lot of parents don't have a good understanding of what it's truly like to be involved in football, particularly at a professional level. As a result, there are many parents who are too vocal and too pushy.

Do you think parents see the career as very glamorous because of what is portrayed in the media?

Callum: Yes, but it's not as glamorous as it looks. If you make it to the very top, then it can be, but if you're anything below the Championship League in England, it's difficult. You might still get paid a decent amount, but you're fighting for your contract to be renewed every year, and if you don't get it, the income you've been on is not life changing. You're effectively fighting for your livelihood every year.

Is there anything else you think parents should perhaps reconsider doing?

Diogo: I have parents of six-year-olds asking me what exercises they can do with them at the park. I always respond with *"How about going to the park to have some quality time together?"* Kick the ball together, take turns having shots at goals, let your child go in goal for a bit, create memories and have fun. Take a ball, not a ball bag, and please leave cones, ladders and poles at home. I have been known to stop working with kids who have parents who refuse to take my advice on this. I know it's not good for the kids in the long run, and I don't feel right contributing to it. It's not helping them, and it's sad.

What do you think parents can do to help their children cope with the emotional rollercoaster of a competitive sport like football, particularly during selection times?

Diogo: That is a tough one. It's tough because it comes down to individuals. I know some kids who are clearly not the best players, but they love it, and they just want to play. I was having a conversation with my nephew once, and he was so excited because he came fifth in his cross country and beat his personal best time. He was so happy, and I thought, *You're the best kid ever!* Another child might come fifth and feel very different. They might be disappointed in themselves. It really depends on each individual child.

How they cope with rejection and what they might need following it can vary. It might be helpful to say things like *"Don't worry, we'll find you another club"* or *"We will try again next year, and in the meantime, we will practise or take you to Diogo at DF and get you some extra technical training"* [Diogo laughs]. It all depends on what your relationship with your child is like and what each parent thinks will work for each child.

What can parents do to support their child during setbacks?
Chloe: Just be there. Support them and tell them there will always be ups and downs in sport. Also, remind them to take something positive out of the situation they're in.

Emily: At this point in my life, I would say to go and play for someone who respects you, believes in you and knows how to get the best out of you. However, I look back on my journey and appreciate the times when I had to stay and fight for a spot too. That's when I learned important lessons. I don't think there's any right or wrong answer. You need to do what you think is best for your child at the time.

During difficult times and football setbacks, having a good support network and something else you can lean into is so important, otherwise you can very easily lose your passion for football and resent it.

What else is important that you think parents should know?
Diogo: I see kids who come to my training centre and I think, *Geez, they've gotten better.* They have gotten better, and they have also developed more confidence and grown into their bodies. These little things can make a big difference. There's a lot of things contributing to personal performance. Parents and players need to be patient.

During your journey, was there anything you asked from your parents to help support you?
Diogo: My parents stopped going out on a Saturday night. I would annoy my parents to get home because I had a game the next day. Also, if people came to our house, I would walk out of my room and ask them to keep the noise down because I needed to get sleep the night before a game. I was only a child when I started doing this, so they must have thought I was crazy.

What values did your parents instil in you that helped during your years as a player?
Diogo: Having a parent who teaches values such as patience, commitment, loyalty and hard work is important. If you work hard and do the right things, opportunities will come.

During my time, regardless of where I was or if things were going well or not, I always worked hard.

I tried not to give anyone any reason not to play me. I never wanted coaches to think, *He's slacking off*. That was me, but I think my parents were my role models because they worked hard.

As a coach now, what I often see with my own team of players is their heads are down at the next training session if they aren't picked to play at an upcoming game. When they do this, it reaffirms I made the right decision not to select them. They have justified my choice. Instead, players should keep working hard, give their best to whatever team they're in, and whatever happens after that happens. It's out of your and your child's control.

What can parents do to help maximise their kids' potential?
Diogo: Kids can get better and maximise their potential, but parents need to understand there're things you can't teach. Things like passion, dedication, desire are all individually innate. You're born with it or you're not. I can imagine it's hard when you see your child has potential and you think they're going to waste their talent. It would be tempting to push them, but you must realise they need to want it themselves. If they don't want to do it themselves, you're wasting your time.

What is the best age to take your child overseas if they are talented enough and scouted?

Diogo: It is different for everyone. All kids mature at different ages, and there are various types of maturity too, like physical maturity, mental and emotional maturity, social maturity and academic maturity. Parents need to assess their own child to see if they are ready. Some may be ready at eighteen. Others may not be ready until they are twenty-four.

What advice have parents sought from you?
Diogo: Sometimes parents approach me and tell me they know I was hard-working and that my mentality was unbelievable as a player, then they ask me if I can have a chat with their child so that they can develop the same habits. I can chat with them, but it's going to go in one ear and out the other. If I had a secret recipe for instilling hard work in people, I would be earning millions, and people would be coming to me from all over the world. This doesn't exist. It's either in you or it's not. That's something that can't be taught.

Do you believe kids need a break or something else besides football?
Callum: Yes, 100 per cent. You need other hobbies. Also, if you stop playing for a little bit, it refuels your love for the game. It's important to give children a break so they can miss it and, consequently, stay in love with the game.

When I was with Liverpool, I would come home on a Saturday after my game and go and watch Manchester United at Old Trafford because I still had a season ticket.

By the time I started training full time, I stopped doing that because the last thing I wanted to do was watch more football after a full week of it. I couldn't stand the thought of football until I was back at training.

That's why when I see football players going away on the weekend or going out with friends, and the next day they are in the papers being accused of 'not being professional', I get a bit annoyed. I don't agree with that. I understand how important it is to get time away to unwind and regain some life balance.

Emily: Parents should encourage their children to have other hobbies outside of football, because eventually, when football is over, it's hard for them to know who they are outside of being a footballer. Even now, I will attend a family function and one of the first things people will ask me is, *"Are you still injured?"* or *"How's football going?"* They mean well, but it's important for athletes to be seen as people outside of football too, because when you don't have an identity outside of your sport, it can become dangerous to your mental health.

A heavy football schedule consisting of seven days a week, for example, is only going to lead them to burnout. Have a healthy balance because when you do, you perform better on the pitch. Yes, I was training a lot on my own, but that was my way of having down time and fun.

Is there anything you think clubs could be doing to better support players?

Adriana: Something clubs could be doing better is providing more transparency. As a player, it's hard not knowing if you're going to get a call back for trials each year, sometimes even after the trial period has long passed. During that waiting period, it feels like you're living in limbo and that's hard. You can't plan your future. That time can feel like forever.

What would you say to your own children if they asked you whether or not they should play football?

Josh: I would say, *"If it's what you want to do and you love it, then pursue it."* There's no greater feeling than doing something you've always wanted to do, and that makes you happy. Then I would prepare them for what the journey might look like. I'd get them to read this book.

One thing my dad always said to me was *"Do whatever you want to do. Just be happy."* I knew I would always have support from my family if I ever wanted to quit or retire and return home to Bunbury. I want to extend that level of support to my children because I imagine there's nothing worse than feeling trapped because your parents are pushing you into doing something you don't want to do.

MAKING IT...OR NOT

Psychologist Lara Faga

Firstly, can you tell us a little bit about your experience working as a psychologist with elite athletes?
Lara: Currently, I'm working with an AFLW (Australian Football League Women's) team within Melbourne. The advice I provide translates to all athletes, regardless of the level they're playing at or sport they have chosen.

What can parents do to help their children who seem nervous during their games?
Lara: When nerves are too high, it can greatly impact performance. Positive self-talk can help in these instances. Players can say to themselves, *"I'm good enough."* Another thing that's really important, and this isn't just for athletes, is to remember that no matter what you want to be successful in, you need to foster a growth mindset. It's all about saying, *"I can't do this yet"* as opposed to *"I can't do this."* This means taking what you can't do yet, setting it as a challenge for yourself, and breaking it down into small bits you can work on, which ultimately leads to gradual improvement.

Most people thrive when they are confident. If they believe in themselves and feel good, their performance is going to improve. Having a good first five minutes of a game means players are more likely to have a solid game overall, because their confidence is high. That is why it's important for players to learn how to calm their nerves down and turn things around during a game, if they aren't playing well.

What would you say to a player who is striving for success in their sport but is experiencing setbacks?
Lara: First and foremost, I'm really big on thinking about the whole person, not just the athlete. This means paying attention to both mental and physical health, the wellbeing of the person. If you're not well, or you're not considering your life overall, then you're not going to succeed as an athlete. I look at an athlete holistically and make sure they are not neglecting relationships, other hobbies, other parts of their life. Time away from football is crucial for optimal mental health and performance.

When people face setbacks, sometimes they think they have to work harder and harder; they have that 'grind' mentality and forget about everything else in order to focus on their sport. Working hard, being determined and disciplined, is obviously important, but not at the expense of other aspects of life.

When a player is well-rounded and can focus on other things, that's when they can rekindle the joy and love for their sport. They enjoy what they're doing and remember why they started playing in the first place. Usually, it's because they love the sport, and it makes them feel a certain way. Once they have connected with that feeling again, performance anxiety drops, and they start to do their best because they're not putting added pressure on themselves.

I talk to athletes about staying in that 'sweet spot'. There needs to be enough stress and pressure to perform at their best but not too much that they collapse, and it becomes overwhelming.

What can parents do to help their kids understand the emotional rollercoaster associated with sports?
Lara: I can answer this through my own experience as a parent and because I work with athletes now, who sometimes describe their childhood and explain how their parents did or didn't support them or currently do or don't support them.

The number one thing is to love your child unconditionally. Support your child regardless of whether they're going through setbacks or not and whatever it is they're striving for. They don't need a parent to be another coach. They need the parent to be a parent, and the child needs to know the parent loves them and accepts them, no matter what.

So, if a child feels they're striving for their parents' approval, that's added pressure on them. A lot of the time I'll hear kids say, *"I just want to make my dad (or mum) proud"* or *"This is what they wanted for me."* Let your child know you love and support them, no matter what, as your child and not as a 'football player'. You don't want them to feel like their achievements correlate with how much you love, appreciate and support them.

As a parent, you're there to listen. You're there to give them a hug. You're there to understand and empathise with them. You're not there to fix the problem or setback on their behalf. You're not there to try and coach them either. You leave that up to the coaches and the professionals. Give them what they need at the time, and bear in mind this can change over time as well.

More specifically, how can parents manage a highly driven child who may get deselected and is struggling with that?
Lara: Parents can help their child connect to their 'why?' Ask them, *"Why do you want to be part of a team? Why is it important for you to do this? How does it make you feel?"* Open their curiosity.

Talking about values is not a concept young kids may understand, but adults do. We understand it's important to live by what we value, then derive our goals from that. Being able to ask our kids why it's so important opens this dialogue.

Having this conversation will help remind children why they play. Usually, it's because they love it, because it makes them smile, or it makes them feel capable. Maybe it's because when they're playing, time stands still and they're in 'the zone' doing something they love.

Sometimes children will look for reassurance from their parents that everything is going to be okay. Talking about why they play helps them understand they can still have that, and that the club or team is irrelevant.

Some kids may feel comfortable connecting with their parents and asking questions, while some may shut down and not want to talk. They might feel like they're going to be criticised by their parents or critiqued. They may be told what to do or what their parents are going to do to fix it. While they need reassurance and guidance, first and foremost, they just need to be heard, loved and understood.

If you let them know all emotions are okay, they'll work through it themselves.

What's your advice for players showing signs of being high achievers?
Lara: When kids are high achievers, that leans into perfectionism, and I think it's important to find out where that comes from.

Why do they feel they need to be perfect or the need to achieve? In most cases, that comes from expectations from parents, whether that's communicated explicitly or implicitly.

Without realising it, parents sometimes show a sense of pride when their child makes it onto an A-team. Kids internalise this and conclude that if they achieve, they will make their parents proud. Remaining neutral and making it clear that as a parent you would've been proud regardless can help. Rather than focus on the result, tell them you are proud of the qualities they displayed; for example, say things like *"I'm so proud that you were really nervous, yet you went out there and you did it"* or *"I'm so proud that it was thirty degrees outside, and although you were feeling hot and tired, you still went out there and played."* It's being proud of the effort they put in. It's being proud of the discipline they show. It's being proud of the qualities they display and the process rather than the outcome.

I think this is changing with our children's generation in comparison to previous generations. I find that children who are high achievers are not just like that with sport. They aim high at school and in other things too.

We all need a level of discipline, motivation and inspiration to do our best and to succeed, but we need to know our self-worth is not based on what we achieve. Kids need to be reminded of that. It's a balance between understanding the importance of trying to achieve goals without being too hard on themselves.

When I work with my athlete clients, we discuss values first, then derive goals from what they value, because the goals become meaningful that way.

The majority of the time, high achievers feel like they will be more accepted and loved the more they achieve.

What can players do to manage their anxiety and performance during trial period?
Lara: There's so much research now around our nervous system and what we can do when we are feeling nervous or stressed. Players can become so anxious about the outcome of the trial that they go into fight, flight, freeze (or fawn) mode. A lot of people think that going into those modes is exclusive to those experiencing a traumatic event, but we know this is not the case. There's a tipping point which varies from person to person. Factors such as temperament, the environment and previous experiences can influence a tipping point.

If a player is too stressed, or they're feeling pressure from parents or coaches or anyone else, they can shut down (freeze/fawn). This means the player may want to curl up in a ball or sleep. They might wonder why they feel so tired before they're about to step onto a pitch. That's the nervous system saying *it's too much or there's danger here, so I need to shut down.*

Others may be bouncing off the walls or get quite aggressive if their body responds to stress by going into fight mode. They might start yelling or be irritable.

Going into any of these defensive, self-preservation modes is a means of avoiding it. They don't want to think about it or may want to skip training.

It's about recognising when the nervous system is overworked due to pressure and anxiety and identifying ways to regulate it. Thankfully, there are several ways players can do that. It can be through breathing, some form of meditation, self-talk, going for a run around the block or playing something other than football. When the nervous system is fired up, talking about it will only get them so far. They have to do something with their body to calm down. That's when they might choose to use strategies such as having a cold shower or splashing cold water on their face.

It's also important to remind them it's not the end of the world if they don't 'make it' and that it's about focusing on the process rather than the outcome.

When players are so fixated on the outcome by thinking *I need to make the team, I need to make this competition* or *I need to win,* that creates a lot of stress. Players can ease their nerves by thinking about the here and now. For example, *What am I doing right now? Am I enjoying myself? What's the next step?* It's not thinking about making the team but rather *I'm kicking the ball right now with my teammate, I'm in a match,* or *I'm in my trials, and I'm just going to focus on my skills and what I can control.* Breaking the process down into little pieces reduces the overwhelm.

Players can't control the outcome, but they can control the process, and if they focus on that, they're going to be less anxious, feel less pressure and enjoy themselves more.

Often, parents give their child advice or try to motivate them in the car on the way to a game. What's your take on these types of conversations?
Lara: It can add more pressure, but it depends on the child and how much reassurance

they need. Make that conversation more about the here and now. It's not about saying, *"You're going to smash it today,"* but more about, *"Go out there, take it moment by moment, and enjoy yourself."* When they enjoy themselves and stay present, their performance is going to be at its best.

With regards to self-talk, we all have a negative and a positive voice. Have a dialogue with your kids around which voice is the loudest. Is it the coaches? Is it the critics? What's the coach telling you? Be that positive voice in your child's head rather than an extra critic because, realistically, they will already have self-doubt in their mind.

I was reading an article recently about a study conducted by a university that states 55 per cent of youth academy players who are dropped or deselected are diagnosed with a mental health condition soon after their release. Why do you think this might be?
Lara: Unfortunately, I don't think the statistics for the non-athlete population are any better. Mental health conditions such as anxiety and depression are on the rise in our youth, particularly with regards to eating disorders. Social media is a big cause of this.

I think one of the biggest factors contributing to poor mental health in athletes is how strongly they link their identity and self-worth to their performance and career. Thoughts like *If I'm not good enough to make this team or if I can no longer play in this team or if I can no longer play due to injury, then I'm worthless.* The players may feel like they don't know who they are because they've always been seen as 'the athlete', and if they can't be that anymore, then they question who's going to love them.

Ultimately, we all want to be loved. We all want to be accepted. From an evolutionary perspective, being ostracised meant death, so we still have that survival mechanism to want to be loved and part of a community.

For children in particular, being told *"You can no longer play with us"* not only makes them believe they are not good enough but also makes them feel a sense of loss and separation from their community. Suddenly, they are on the outside, and without really knowing it, the primal part of their brain subconsciously equates that to death.

It's the whole idea that *if I'm out on my own, if I don't belong, I can't survive. I need belonging. I need a community, a village. If I don't belong here, where do I belong?*

This takes me back to what I mentioned earlier about what parents can do. Reminding their child they belong within their family, no matter what that family looks like, is important. It reassures them they have a place, and they don't need their football team to feel like they belong somewhere. If a child is raised with that sense of belonging and self-worth and unconditional love, then when that child becomes an adult athlete, they will look after the other aspects of their life, and the statistics may not be so high.

THE PARENTS' ROLE

Sometimes players feel like they don't have the time to dedicate themselves to other things should a football career not work out. What advice do you have?

Lara: Knowing you have to put everything into football, and therefore, don't have the time, energy or resources for other things can be the reality of an elite athlete. However, it's important to maintain the mindset that once this is done, I will do all these other things, rather than once this is done, then what? I'm nothing. Acknowledging they can be a footballer for a particular time in their life—when they are young, healthy and the opportunity is there to be grabbed with both hands—is important, but so is preparing for when that time is over. It might be to study or to start a business or to have a family. Knowing that playing at an elite level is not forever and there are other things players may want to pursue can make all the difference.

What can parents do to help their children maintain a love for their sport, particularly after many setbacks?

Lara: Parents need to think about their own agenda first. Do you want them to continue to love the sport because you love it or because you've already invested so much time and money into it and your child is good at it? There are many sports out there, so children don't need to be restricted to one. If the child loved a certain sport once but doesn't anymore, yet the parent is insisting they continue to play, then that may be the parent's ego at play.

When you initially asked the question, my first response was, how do you continue to ensure your child maintains a love for life? How are you fostering healthy relationships within the family and within friendship groups? How are you getting them out in nature? How are you getting your child to enjoy unstructured time and moving their bodies when they're not on the pitch?

Children may not follow or love their sport throughout their lives. They may burn out; they may have started too young, and they don't love it anymore. What's important is how they continue to love to move their body, have real-life connections and relationships. Thinking about how you can foster a life for them where they don't feel the need to escape and isolate themselves is a better way of approaching it.

Apart from having positive physical and mental health benefits, what are some other benefits to playing a sport that you think parents should know?

Lara: I often hear the term 'put your kids in sports so they stay off the streets'. There is some truth to that. Sport can deter kids from spending too much time gaming in isolated bedrooms, doing drugs or being on the streets.

Sport gives an athlete a certain respect for their body and mind, and it can create a sense of community. Instead of finding that on the streets, a child or youth player can find it in a team.

What do you think would help coaches get the best out of their teams?
Lara: I think what's really important for coaches is to understand they are working with a whole group of individuals. Some will respond well to an aggressive approach and have that *'I'll show you'* mentality, but others shut down. A coach should be invested in their players as people and get to know each individual to better understand how to interact with them one-on-one.

The relationship between a coach and a player is a two-way street, but the more that relationship is fostered, the more the coach is going to understand how the player responds to feedback, what motivates them and what deflates them, and approach them accordingly.

The coach I work with at an elite level may say to me, *"Lara, I have to give information to a player. how do you think I should approach them?"* If available, I highly recommend relying on resources, such as a team psychologist or a physiotherapist who knows the player well, to gain as much information as possible. What motivates Player A is not what's going to motivate Player B.

As a group, it can be difficult to address everybody in the way they need, so if a coach's post-game style after a loss, let's say, is to let off steam and be aggressive, I would suggest they avoid giving feedback when they have heightened emotions. Just like players need to regulate their emotions, coaches need to regulate theirs as well. Most people don't respond well to being yelled at, put down or criticised.

Coaches need to learn different communication styles. When they address a team, they may have a certain style and think it's the right one to motivate their team, but they need to check in constantly because there are different dynamics within a team, and as the years go on, players come and go. There are different maturity levels too. When talking to children, they can't process any form of being yelled at or told off. That's not going to be helpful.

There is some responsibility on the players to understand the coach's style as well. When a coach yells, they should remind themselves not to take it personally because they're simply letting off steam. Remember that they mean well, and they just want the best for the team.

Let's Talk Football

Now that you have read the book, why don't you have a chat with your parents or a teammate about football. See how you go answering and talking about these questions. Have fun and enjoy realising how much you've learned from the amazing players you just read about.

Why do you play football?
What are some of the things you love about playing?
Is there anything you don't like about football?
Do you want to play football for a hobby, or would you like it to become your career?
After reading this book do you understand you will probably experience many ups and downs and that's okay?
What are some of the great things you may experience?
What are some bad things you may experience?
If you ever feel like the pressure is getting too much, what are some things you can do to help yourself?
What can you do to help a teammate who may be going through a tough time in football?
Apart from football, what else do you enjoy doing?
Do you know that if football doesn't become your career, you can still enjoy playing?
Where do you think you could play and have fun?

Acknowledgements

What started out as a quick journal entry to overcome a personal experience soon turned into a book. A real book. A book I never thought possible. I want to thank the following people who supported an idea I came up with one uneventful afternoon, which turned into a dream that became a reality.

First and foremost, my three sons, Jai, Levi and Dion. I want to thank you for being the inspiration behind this book. There were many times when I could've, perhaps should've, taken you to the park or played a game of Monopoly with you, but instead was working on 'the book'. I appreciate your patience and hope the fact that I have now mentioned your names in 'the book' has made it all worthwhile.

Jai and Levi. Thank you for giving me your honest opinion when I sought your advice on different aspects of the book. I apologise for stealing from your library to look at page numbers and font sizes, etc. You can have your books back now.

Dion. The posters displayed across many soccer clubs throughout Victoria and on social media platforms offering an opportunity to register for pre-sales were designed by none other than my nine-year-old son, Dion. Son, your future is looking bright.

Andrew. Where do I even start? You've constantly supported me, brainstormed with me (sometimes at ridiculous hours), and used your business and technology expertise to fulfil my requests. None of this has gone unnoticed. You did an amazing job with the website, and the design of the player profile pages have been given a big thumbs up by me and the players. Your numerous talents and your intelligence continues to astound me.

Mum and Dad. Thank you for always being my biggest supporters. Without that unconditional love and support, life becomes that little bit more difficult, and projects as large as this are much harder to fulfil. Dad, you can let all your soccer fanatic friends at your seniors clubs know that the book you've been bragging about is finally done. Yes, Mum told me. Thanks Mum, and thanks for sharing each exciting moment with me.

ACKNOWLEDGEMENTS

My mother- and father-in-law. Thank you for your patience while I've spent many of our Thursday nights with my head buried in my laptop, looking up from time to time to ask if a particular paragraph reads well. Your willingness to listen and support in any way you can hasn't gone unnoticed.

Mary Lynn. A massive thank you to Mary Lynn, my editor from the Leadership Literary Lab. You have an admirable eye for detail. Your ability to tweak a sentence into something incredibly captivating is your superpower. I can't thank you enough for guiding me step by step throughout the entire process. A process that was new to me. You saw the potential in this book from day one, agreed to run at my pace, never gave up on me, and made sure I never doubted myself or the book. The success of this book, whether big or small, is something I celebrate in partnership with you.

Jason. I truly appreciate our shared passion for getting this book into the hands of as many players as possible. You see the value in it as much as I do, and for that I'm so glad you are part of the team. Congratulations on your own best-selling book success. Now that I know what it takes to write a book, I realise the extent of that achievement. I do apologise for you having to stay awake until 'stupid o'clock' to attend virtual meetings. You have your nights back now.

Bonita Mersiades and the team at Fair Play Publishing. Thank you for taking a chance on this book. I truly appreciate it and hope it has the positive impact on the football community we are hoping for.

Lara, the trusted psychologist with a wealth of knowledge in the sporting industry. I loved every minute of our chat. I want to thank you from the bottom of my heart for providing the readers with the information we so desperately needed. Parents now know how to best support their young players, and coaches have a better understanding on how to get the best out of their players, all because of you. I also appreciate you introducing me to a café that makes a really good chai latte.

The players. The talented idols that are the players featured in this book:

Melissa and Adriana Taranto. What a delight you two are! I will always cherish the day we bonded over a macchiato at a local café where you so openly shared your journeys. We laughed a lot, and if my memory serves me well, there were many moments when I couldn't fit a word in, and I love that.

Josh Risdon. You opened up for the benefit of others without a second thought. I will never forget the moment you said, "I think this book is amazing, and there needs to be more of it because I had no idea going into it what the journey was truly like, and I wish that I did." My eyes welled up, and I knew at that moment, no matter how challenging it was going to get, I needed to see this book through. Another thing that amazes me is how grounded you are despite your level of success.

Chloe Logarzo. I have never met someone who speaks with so much passion in her voice. Thank you for being an open book, supporting this venture, and teaching us all that no matter how many times you're knocked down, you can make a comeback. You inspire so many players and your Future Baller initiative is just the beginning of amazing things to come. On a side note, I still giggle when I remember your reaction to the bird that flew into the café. Priceless.

Emily Gielnik. To all six foot of you. Given my height, or lack thereof, I'm so glad I was sitting down when we met. Thank you for sharing your story, one that is not traditional. It gives aspiring players hope when things aren't going to plan. Your resilience and 'never-give-up' attitude is a force to be reckoned with. You're incredibly talented and any players who join your Future Baller clinic are in for an experience that's going to put them in good stead for whatever their future looks like.

Callum Nicholas. The boy from Manchester. Given the statistics, your story is the one that is going to resonate with many players, and for that, I am grateful you shared it. I want you to know your willingness to reveal every detail of your football journey, your level of resilience and your ability to pivot when things didn't quite turn out as you planned are inspiring. I have so much belief in you! Continue to enjoy your current adventures and know that the best is yet to come. Once again, I apologise for the blunt knives at the restaurant we ate at.

Last but certainly not least, 'D' (Diogo Ferreira). You probably don't know this, but you were the first person I reached out to when I had the crazy idea to write this book. From day one, you were one of my biggest supporters. For that, I'm forever grateful. Without any hesitation, you gave me the confidence I needed to pursue this idea, because you saw first-hand how much this book was needed, then continued to help me in many other ways too. Whether it was to put me in contact with other players, or to hang up some posters at your academy, no request was off limits. You were the first person I interviewed, and although you got lettuce on my phone, it was one of the most enjoyable lunches I have had. I love how you value honesty above all else, and because of this, you have the potential to become one of the most respected coaches this country has produced.

About the Author

Amy Schembri is from Melbourne where she lives with her husband and three sons.

She spends the majority of her time at a football pitch supporting her boys while they play. When not embarrassing them by yelling out "Great pass" or "Take a shot" from the sidelines, she has a nine-to-five job in Human Resources. She also likes to bury her head in a good book or attempt to keep her home in good order.

Doing what she can to soften the blow of de-selection and the pressures associated with the game from such a young age has become her passion.

MORE
REALLY GOOD FOOTBALL
BOOKS FROM
FAIR PLAY PUBLISHING

Available from

fairplaypublishing.com.au

and all good bookstores

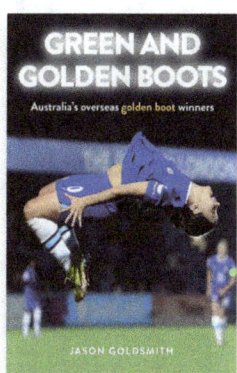
Green and Golden Boots

Socceroos – A World Cup Odyssey, 1965 to 2022 Volumes 1 and 2

The Agents' Game

The Aboriginal Soccer Tribe

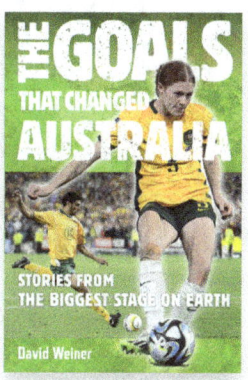
The Goals That Changed Australia

The First Matildas

Hear Us Roar – An anthology of emerging women football writers

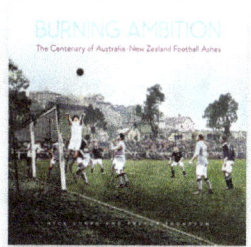
Burning Ambition

www.fairplaypublishing.com.au

www.ingramcontent.com/pod-product-compliance
Lightning Source LLC
Chambersburg PA
CBHW050244120526
44590CB00016B/2207